Voices of America

Boonton

Voices of America

Boonton

Compiled by
Arthur Rabin

ARCADIA
PUBLISHING

ISBN 978-0-7385-0528-2

Published by Arcadia Publishing
Charleston, South Carolina

Printed in the United States of America

Library of Congress Catalog Card Number: 2001086558

For all general information contact Arcadia Publishing at:
Telephone 843-853-2070
Fax 843-853-0044
E-Mail sales@arcadiapublishing.com
For customer service and orders:
Toll-Free 1-888-313-2665

Visit us on the Internet at www.arcadiapublishing.com

Contents

Every community has a history which, if properly related, must be interesting and even important at least to those who belong to it. Here the fathers of such a community fought the battle of life, wrestled with the problems of moral responsibility, loved the living, pitied the sorrowful, helped the weak, wept over the dying; here they laid the foundation of a social fabric as best they could, often in a very blind but honest method, lived life as we now live it, and they died leaving their graves to us as silent monitors not to permit them to sink into forgetfulness. Although not as great as many who have lived, they are our forefathers, and the work they did for us merits a grateful record at our hands.

—Rev. Joseph Farrand Tuttle of the Rockaway
Presbyterian Church, 1847–1862

PREFACE

Before written history existed, oral history was the way humans learned about their past. Stories of family traditions and the exploits of tribal heroes were handed down from generation to generation. In many parts of the world, this is how societies still learn about their past.

As humans began to write, and later with the invention of the printing press, written history became the conduit for the past. That history was made up almost exclusively of the stories of royalty and aristocrats whose ancestors were their only credentials. In these chronicles little happened, or mattered, that did not pertain to those of privileged birth. Other members of society—the nameless and faceless who fought the wars, carried out the orders and often blunders, or were wounded or died in the battles of the privileged class, those who stayed at home, had families, and worked in the fields, stables, and workshops—have vanished into the past without a trace. Women hardly mattered at all.

Today, our study of history is expanding with a revival of interest in the oral tradition. Ordinary and not-so-ordinary men and women have discovered their voice in history and rediscovered their past. Their memories and observations of the times in which they lived have been increasingly recorded. Furthermore, since World War II and the growth of tape recorder technology, the study of oral history has exploded.

From musty attics and basements, old letters, diaries, and fading photographs, formerly consigned to the dustbins of history, have emerged, providing fresh and illuminating perspectives on our past. There are heroes and heroines to whom we point with pride. There are skeletons in our closets as well. As we dig deeper, we may encounter a renegade, a ne'er-do-well, perhaps a criminal perched on a branch of the family tree. That, too, is part of our history.

The past is not written in stone. At one time, the sun was thought to have revolved around a flat earth. It is important to point out that oral history, like written history, to a greater or lesser degree, is a mix of fact and myth, reality and illusion. In *Boonton,* as with all oral history, one cannot vouch for the accuracy or authenticity of all of the stories one hears. Memories dim. Tendencies to embroider or exaggerate must be considered, and some stories are passed down with losses of detail and nuance.

Despite these limitations and qualifications, it seems self-evident that the more information we have from all sources will lead to a better understanding of the past and a better basis for judgments about our future. Clearly oral history has let some fresh air into the study of our past. I hope this book will make a modest contribution to that end.

A word or two about our interviewees. Most of them have roots in the community that go far back; some are comparatively new arrivals. A few live in Boonton Township, have spent much of their time in Boonton, and feel passionately about it, one way or another, as is evident in their voices.

Finally, a personal note. I want to thank you, my hosts, the people of Boonton, who have invited me into your homes and your lives. Your stories have taken me on a journey of discovery about what it has meant and means to be a Boontonite, or as others refer to themselves, Boontonian. Whichever you prefer, it has been a pleasure meeting you.

CHAPTER ONE
THE PEOPLE

Boonton was roaring in the '20's. Barber poles twirled, mills spun silk, a Main Street theater featured two live shows a day and Jersey City resident, Luigi Scerbo, a 22-year-old Italian immigrant, moved to town with his wife, Rose, and infant daughter, Tess.

—From the *Daily Record*, March 18, 1999

In 1919 I was living in Jersey City, but I had a girlfriend in New York. I saw her when I was making deliveries with my horse and wagon. I thought she was very nice, so I used to go and visit her by bus.

And then we got married in 1920 in Our Lady of Mount Carmel. Before we got married we had to go to confession. My grandfather would not let me and my fiancée go by ourselves. We had to be chaperoned. He sent my wife's uncle, Tony, to go with us. But we went back to Jersey City because I was making $18 a week delivering the hay and the oats for the horses on the farm. I couldn't make that kind of money in Boonton. But my wife wanted to live in Boonton close to her family. And the only job I could get here was running a poolroom for my father's cousin, Al Maraziti, who could only pay me $10 a week. I didn't think I could make it [on that salary], but Al came up with another proposition. If I could take care of the furnace and do some other janitor work he would give me an extra few dollars.

So in front of the poolroom I sold hot dogs, soda, and candy. And I had two chairs where I used to shine shoes, 10¢ a shine, and I worked the cash register for the poolroom. Al Maraziti owned the poolroom and the building. Later we lived in an apartment there.

I was making $40 at that time with some help from my father-in-law, who was a good guy. He was honest as the day is long. He would come up loaded with food, because he had a farm.

—Luigi Scerbo

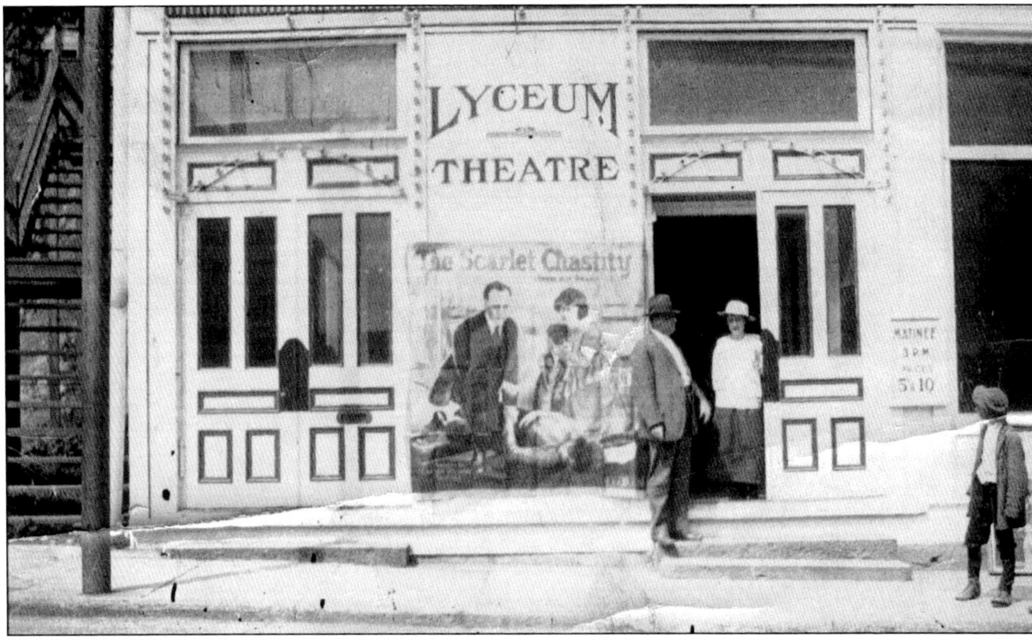

The Lyceum Theatre.

It was the 1920's and actors, such as George Burns, would duck out of nearby Lyceum Theater to shoot a few billiard games and chat between shows.

[Burns would] have a hot dog and a big glass of root beer and then he'd go back and work the matinees in the afternoon. He was a nice guy.

In the evening, shoppers from Denville would alight from a trolley that stopped at Main and Division Streets and stroll downtown. Few people had cars. While window-shopping, people would often stop to watch the canal boats. They cruised down a North Main canal before unloading cargo at the Plane Street incline."

—From the *Daily Record*, March 18, 1999

All in all, we had a good life here in Boonton. I was happy I came here.

—Luigi Scerbo

In 1936, Scerbo and Nick Bevacqua opened the Reservoir Tavern. Numerous plaques hang in the vestibule, representing the dozens of times the restaurant has been chosen by *New Jersey Magazine* for having the best pizza in the state.

—From the *Daily Record*, March 18, 1999

I called Mr. Scerbo one day and I spoke to his daughter, Rose Carey. I said, "I happened to be reading the American Legion magazine and I noticed an article on the veterans of World War I."

I [had] read that surviving members of those who served in France were about to receive a medal from the French government. I asked his daughter, "Did your father go overseas to France in World War I?" And she said, "He sure did." "Do you have his papers?"

"Yes, I do," she said, "we have all of them." "Would you mind if I send them down to the French Embassy in Washington?"

And, lo and behold, they had some people from the French Embassy come down here to Boonton. It's a beautiful medal. And he's about 103 years old. That's something!

—Stephen Bolcar

On September 20, 1999, Luigi Scerbo was named Chevalier of the National Order of the Legion of Honor, the highest French award bestowed upon those who served in World War I.

—From the *Daily Record*, March 18, 1999

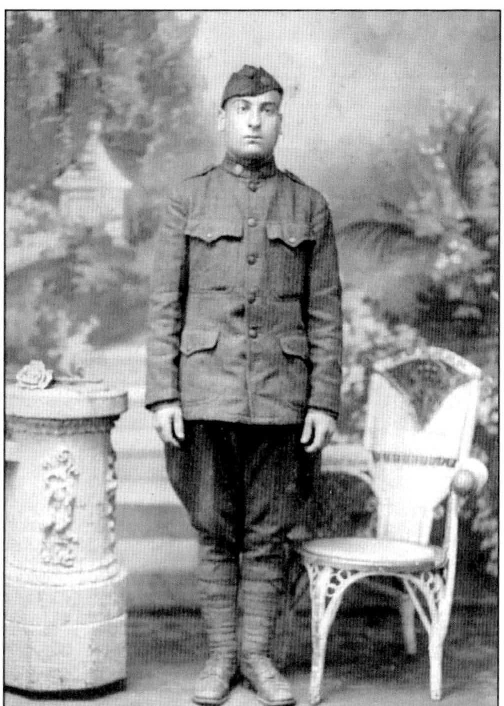

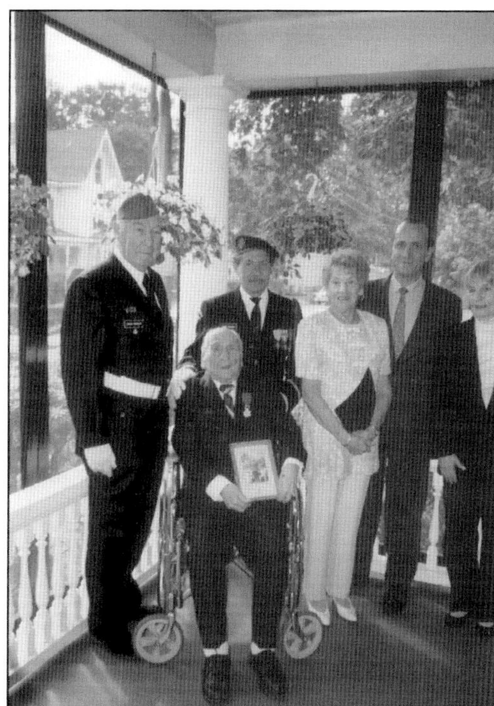

Left: *Luigi Scerbo, a 19-year-old private, shown in 1917.* Right: *Scerbo accepting his award as Chevalier of the National Order of the French Legion of Honor.*

Our father was born here. His original home was 319 Boonton Avenue. Our family was always here. Our grandmother lived across the street, our aunts and uncles and cousins too. [Laughs.] It was a very nice town, simple, quiet. People worked very hard. There were no affluent people. They were all hardworking and supporting big families. Most of the people worked in factories of some kind. We had ironworks and the Boonton Molding Company, E.F. Drew, which was a butter works, Van Raalte Hosiery, Boonton Pocketbook Factory, and all those precision instrument places that made a lot of war products.

—Julia Dunn

There were many people who commuted each day. If you wanted a real job, you had to go to New York. About 500 a day went to the city . . .

—Irene Dunn

. . . by the Delaware and Lackawanna Railroad. [Laughs.]

—Irene and Julia, together

Or teach. You might teach around here. We loved growing up here. When we were children we had a baseball diamond in the backyard. My brothers played baseball. No nice, pretty grass. It was just a place for the guys to play. And the girls, we played jacks. [Laughs.] But, you know, we did chores. There were chores in those days! Remember! [Laughs.] Nobody made a point of entertaining you. Leisure was not like it is now. Our parents didn't have any leisure time. They did like to play cards. People had card parties in their homes. Maybe two tables. They would meet every Sunday night. So we got to know our parents' friends. They were our friends. They played euchre. [Laughs.] Five hundred—whist. No, we didn't play for money. Just for the fun of it.

—Julia

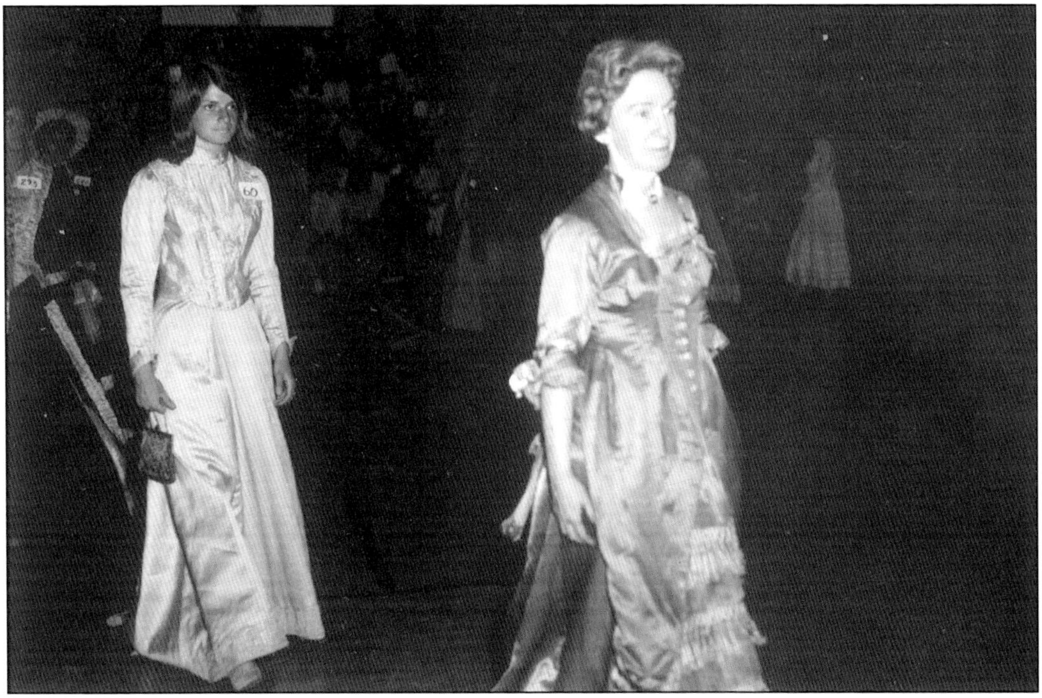

Julia Dunn, right, at the centennial celebrations.

Pop was very civic-minded. He was on boards—Board of Aldermen, Morris County Welfare Board. He was one of the original members of that. And the head of the fire department. Now his grandson is the head of the fire department.

—Irene

We had very simple pleasures, you know. We were happy little kids. And we did a lot of walking. Oh my, did we walk! We walked because there was no other way to go. If you wanted to see any of your friends, you walked, whether they lived over in west Boonton or down the other end of town. You had to walk. If you were taken to Radio City in New York or something, that was a great thing.

—Julia

My grandfather, John Charlton, was born in Hull, England, in 1835. I'm not sure when he came here, but it was early enough so that he fought in the Civil War. My mother's family name was Salmon. The Salmons were originally Scottish. One of them was knighted by Sir Robert Bruce in the 14th century. At some time during the Highland Wars, the Salmon family moved from Scotland and settled in Southwold in England. There were three Salmon brothers who came to America with their families in 1635. I believe one of them went up to Massachusetts, another founded the town of Southhold on Long Island, and the third settled near what is now Elizabeth, New Jersey. My great-grandfather was the Democratic [U.S.] senator of New Jersey in 1898.

—Lloyd Charlton

Anyone who has ever labored behind a horse-drawn plow on a hot summer day could understand how Joshua S. Salmon felt during his childhood on a farm in Bartley: "I do not intend to do this kind of work always," he told a friend. "I believe I am capable of something different than breaking up this stony land."

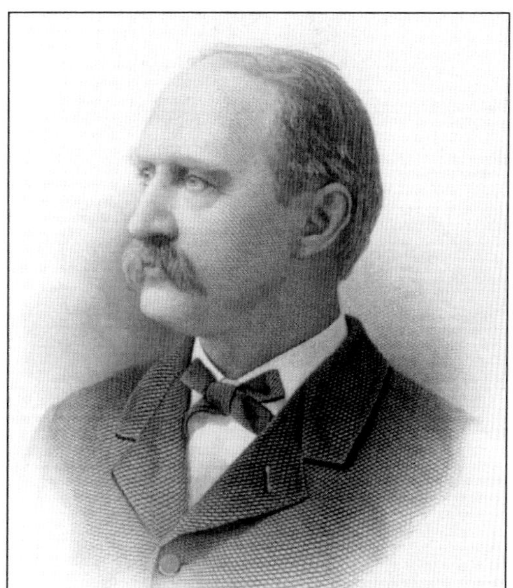

Joshua S. Salmon.

All of which is one way of saying that not even his father's wishes could keep Joshua Salmon down on the farm. He was determined to seek his fortune elsewhere—and this he did, by eventually moving to Boonton.

Salmon was born in 1846 in Mount Olive, grew up on his father's farm in Bartley, and determined at an early age to become "a lawyer and a statesman." After service in the state legislature, Salmon was elected to Congress in 1900 as a Democrat. As a Congressman, Salmon drew a bead on the hottest issues of the day—the tariff and big business. "I believe in equal rights to all and special privileges to none. One of our political parties favors special privileges by taxing the many for the support of the few. The present tariff gives large fortunes to the few by taxing the many. Its main purpose is to increase the wealth of those already rich by robbing the poor.

"Other deplorable conditions exist. Trusts and monopolies prey upon the people. There are and can be no good trusts."

The Congressman blamed the Standard Oil Company for a rise in the price of oil from 6¢ a gallon to "10 or 11¢."

Joshua Salmon died in 1902, not long after he had been nominated for a second term in Congress. The funeral services, they said, were the largest attended of any ever held in Boonton.

—From *The Boonton Years 1867 to 1967*, compiled for the Boonton Centennial Committee

Two years ago my son and a Salmon who lives up in the Ledgewood area decided it was time to start a new family reunion. They wrote to as many [family members] as they could find, and 185 people showed up. So, you see, we spawned a lot of Salmon here. My mother and father were both born here in Boonton. A story that was passed down is that when my grandfather lived on the 200 block of West Main Street, he moved to the 300 block because the landlord decided to raise the rent $10 a month and my grandfather wouldn't pay that outrageous amount. He had a trucking business which started with a team of horses and wagons and then went into motorized trucks. My dad once drove a team of horses and a wagon to Brooklyn to move a family to Boonton, which must have taken several days. He was pretty tough.

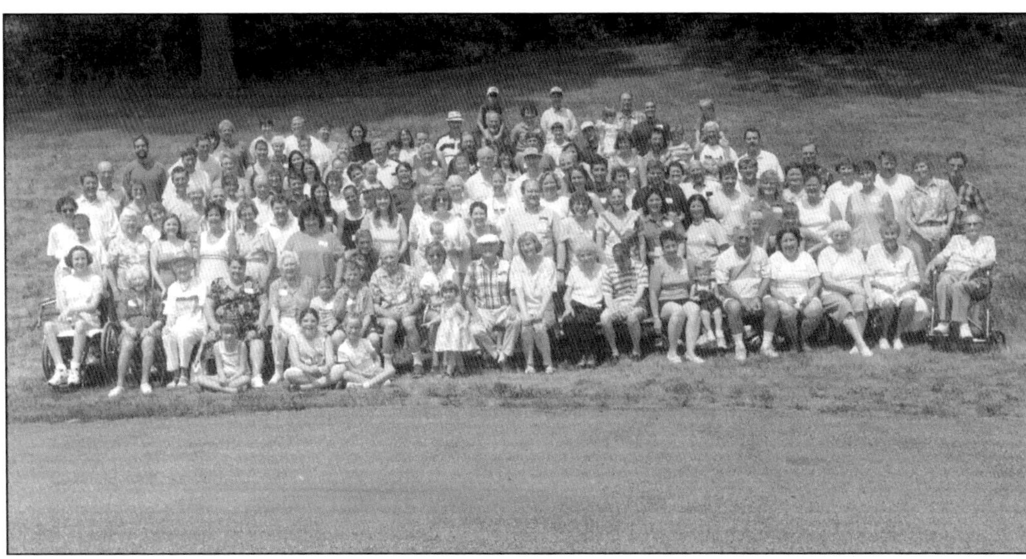

The Salmon family reunion, off Salmon Lane in Edgewood, in July 1999.

We were in church one Sunday morning. We were standing singing a song, my dad, mom, and me, when suddenly my dad collapsed. I yelled out, "Is there a doctor here?"

There was an obstetrician in the congregation and he rushed over, and the minister came down from the pulpit. In the meantime, my dad came to and sat up. Somebody in the back called the Kiwanis Indian Squad ambulance, and when they came they wheeled the stretcher down the aisle. They wanted to put him on it and wheel him out. "No," he said, "I walked in here and I'm going to walk out." And he did.

—Lloyd Charlton

I was born in 1920 in the Shenandoah Valley of Virginia. My grandfather, a minister, called it "God's country." My mother was a teacher and my father was a carpenter. When we first came to Boonton we were housed at the Tomack Motel in Parsippany by the Fair Housing Group. They were affiliated with Bell Labs at the time, where my husband worked. They were anxious for us to find a place to live. Our being black [made it] a hard time for us because this was in [19]66. We were at the motel for six weeks. Very nice accommodations and everyone was exceptional.

Now here I was with a child of five years old and a teenage daughter who had adopted us in New Mexico. [Laughs]. She was our baby-sitter and she said, "If you're going away, I'm going with you." Her parents were saying that after you graduate high school, "You have to get out and get work," but I was saying she had to go to school. She did a year at the University of New Mexico at my insistence.

In New Jersey we were wandering around trying to find a place to live. Wherever we went they told us someone else is being considered. Then a white couple from Fair Housing would go, and they would say, "When do you want to move in?" It was something we expected, because that reaction was universal at the time. It wasn't anything new. We found that in Virginia and New Mexico where we lived. It was a fact of life everywhere. But this was [19]66 now, and we figured it's got to get better. It can't get worse.

Finally we heard about a new development in a town called Boonton. I didn't know anything about Boonton, but we learned they were building up an area called Sunset Lake. We moved in there. My son, Tommy, was five. I had to see if I could enroll him in

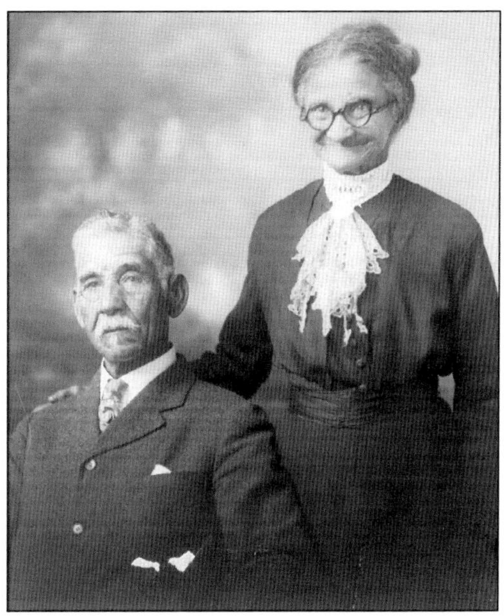

Louada Layton Ramsey's grandparents, Benjamin Thomas Layton, a minister, and Alma Booker Layton, a teacher.

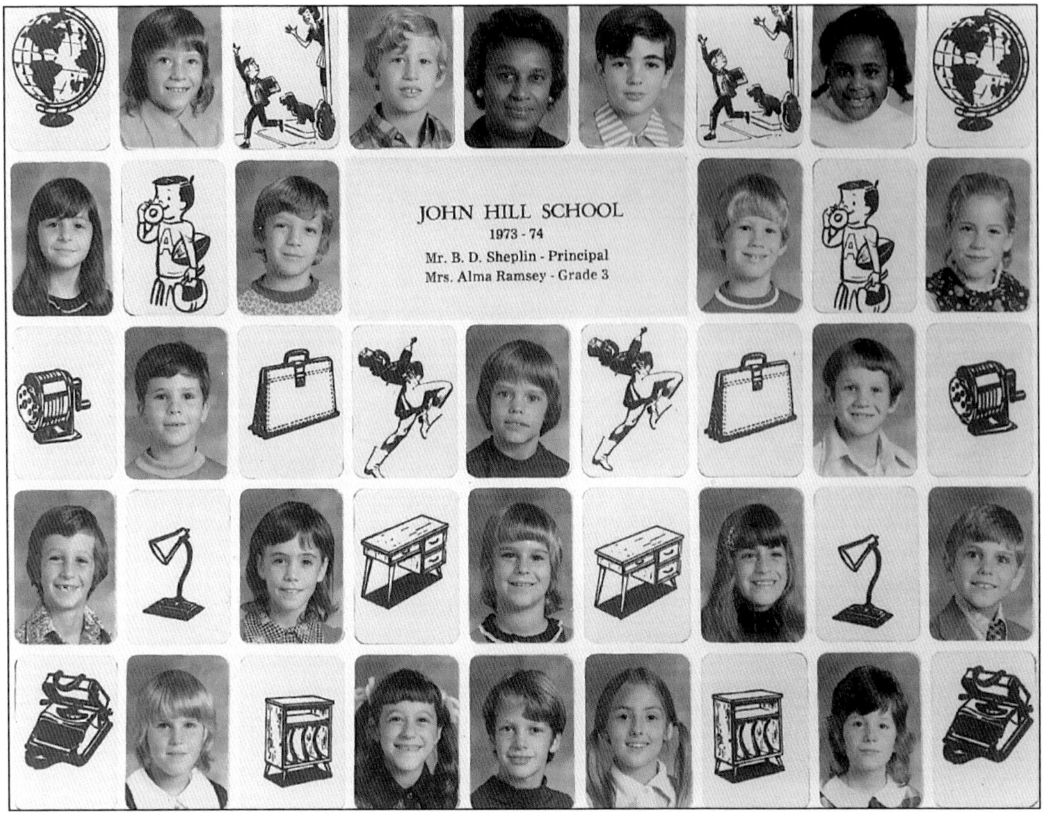

Louada Layton Ramsey's 1973–1974 third-grade class at the John Hill School.

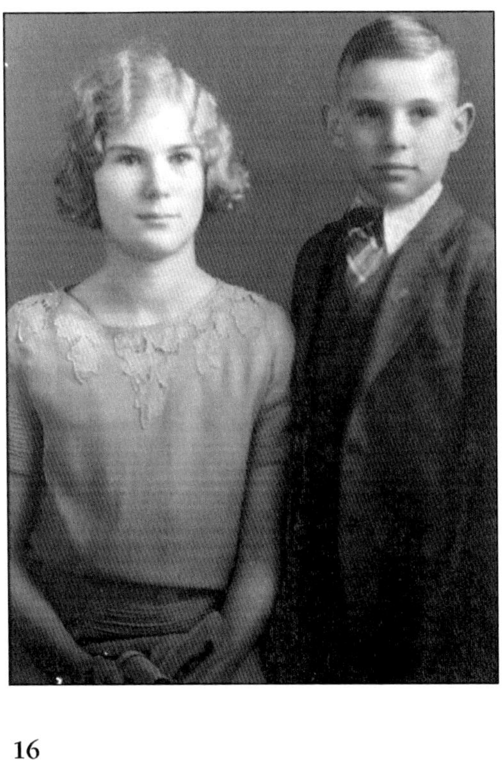

Twelve-year-old Jane Hopkins and her nine-year-old brother, Louis.

kindergarten. I thought we had such a hell of a time finding a place to live, I'm going to the board of education and see if they need a teacher. Though I was a little nervous how they would feel about a black teacher, they hired me. And Mr. Sheplin, the principal, was happy with my work, and I had no problems with the parents and the children.

In fact some of the parents went to Mrs. Fowler, the kindergarten teacher, and said, "I want Mrs. Ramsey for my child's teacher next term."

At Thanksgiving time I would have a quiet time in the morning when I would ask the class just to stop whatever they were doing and think. I was careful about using the word prayer, as I didn't know if that would be acceptable, but I would ask the class to think about what we want to do and how we are going to act today. Many of the parents still remember that the kids would come home and say, "You know, before we do anything in school, we have a quiet time. We're supposed to think."

—Louada Layton Ramsey

My father was a hosiery knitter, which was probably the main industry here at the time. It was one of the few industries that was constantly in one place or another during the Depression. They made silk stockings and there was a great demand for it. My father had followed the trade from upper New York State and the southern tier.

I was born during the Depression, and this was when the hosiery knitters moved around a lot. They were coming from all over the country. When my father came to Boonton he thought it was going to be temporary. For those who lived in Boonton it was a job, but for those who came from all over the country it was a trade.

After my father came here he was working a five-day week and then it was cut to four days, then three days, but there didn't seem like there was any other place to go at the time. Actually before he came to Boonton he was working in Paterson. You know these companies get up a softball or a baseball team, and this time the Paterson team was going to play the Boonton team. After they came up here to play they discovered that nobody had brought a ball. So they had to ride uptown to get a ball.

Anyway, when my father went home that night, he said to my mother, "Mae, you should see that town of Boonton. The whole Main Street is on a hill. I never saw a town with a Main Street on a hill." Little did he know he was going to live out his life here.

—Jim Monaghan

I was at Columbia University in New York. I had a very good friend in Boonton. I thought it was a nice, little town, but I never planned to stay here. But while I was here my friend tried to set up a double date with me. And she met Thomas, who was single. She told him, "I've got a girl I want you to meet." And he said, "Oh, hell, not another one." And she said, "You don't have to worry about this one. She's not interested in getting married. She's going to school and she's interested in getting a position."

So she set up the date. When we met we liked each other, but I really wasn't interested in getting married. To be truthful I had just finished up a very lengthy episode from the army, which I had not really gotten over. Anyway, we met and went together. He was a fine person. He was 33 and I was 30, and so we were at an age when we really knew what we wanted to do, and neither of us wanted to get married.

We went together for four or five months, and he wanted to give me a ring and I wasn't interested in a ring at that stage, so I said, "No." And then the Korean War started and his unit was called. And I was also in the reserve. He really wanted to get married, and I thought, "This is kind of stupid." I liked him, and I was 30 years old and life isn't always peaches and cream, but he was as good a peach as you can find. So we got married before he went to Korea. And I've been a Boontonian ever since.

—Jane Hopkins

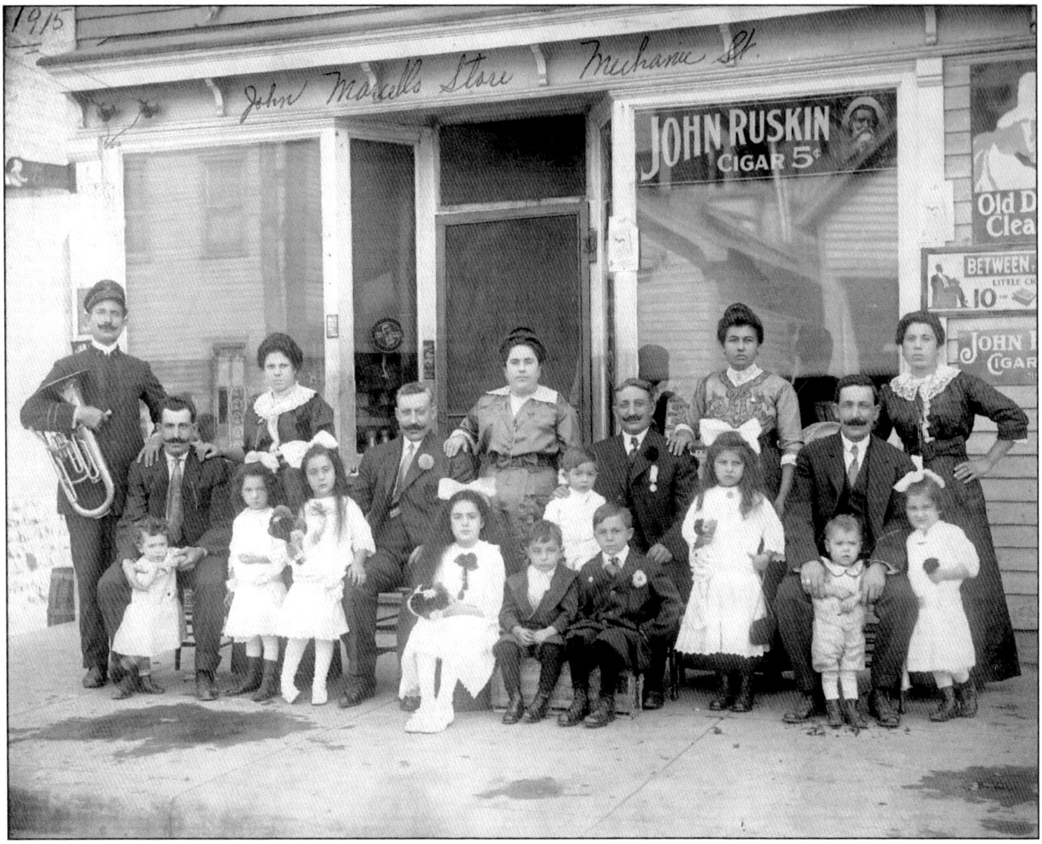

The Marcello brothers and family, c. *1915.*

Pop and his brother John came to America together. In later years, the other three brothers, James, Anthony, and Peter joined them in the U.S. The voyage in steerage was 12 dollars. When they arrived in New York, they were taken to a bleak place of real estate in New York Harbor called Ellis Island. They took their places in long lines and went submissively through the routine of answering interpreters' questions and receiving medical examinations. Four thousand newcomers were processed daily with over half of them having to stay overnight. After this, they were permitted to pass through America's gateway.

Their names were spelled Marciellieo. The immigration department simplified their name and told them from now on their name would be Marcello.

Crossing the harbor on the ferry and gazing at the New York skyline just flabbergasted the two brothers, Joseph and John. It was a new world of fantasy. When they saw their first black man, they just couldn't take off their eyes off him.

Along with their hand baggage, they boarded a marvelous train to Tuxedo Park, New York, where they soon were employed as gardeners. After a few years, my father decided to return to his home in Italy. He had become disillusioned with "the Land of Opportunity." He had to work twelve hours a day, six or seven days a week, for an average of less than 10 dollars. He had been irresistibly drawn here by the conviction that in America he would find what the Old Country had denied him. He returned to his native land, leaving his older brother, John, here in America.

A few months after his return to Italy, his brother John wrote to tell him that a dam was going to be constructed creating the Jersey City reservoir. The stone was to be quarried in Montville and they could use all the help they could get. Pop married Mom, Ernestine Lambiase, during his stay in Italy and brought her back along with him to America on their honeymoon. They came back to this country via Ellis Island, and came to Montville, New Jersey. Pop, eventually, became a foreman at the quarry where he and many other Italians cut the rock that was used to build the reservoir dam in the early 1900's. The same stone was used around 1860 to build Our Lady of Mt. Carmel Church in Boonton.

Mom came to America with joy in her heart at the age of sixteen, because in Italian montville means "village in the mountains." Much to her surprise, she found a shack made from crates and boxes waiting for her with other Italians from all parts of Italy, living in a hell hole.

She cried for a year wanting to return to her native land. The area they lived in was called Hog Mountain. The problems were many. Knifings, killings, and fights created many hardships. No doctor would enter the village and they couldn't get ice and other supplies either. The Italians were not allowed in Boonton. My mother always sympathized with the Negroes' problems of equality, because she remembered when her people weren't allowed to enter Boonton because of discrimination. Later they were the first Italians to move into Boonton onto Mechanic Street, where they would open a grocery store and raise eight children. The first, of a total of nine, died at an early age. All nine children were born without the assistance of a doctor. . . .

Boonton had a beautiful nucleus of people. We all tended to ourselves and grew up speaking the language of our forefathers and living with their customs. But it was the mixture of these peoples that made this country what it is today. It took many years before these people would intermarry with other nationalities. It took World War II to straighten that out because we fought next to Jews, Poles, Swedes, blacks, and the like. This made us all one.

Pop had come to America because it was a growing country which was called the Land of Opportunity. Its streets were said to be lined with gold. Most immigrant families had firmly believed they would actually pick gold up off the streets. When they settled here, they finally realized that the only way they were going to make money was to work for it. Most of them had little education and they ended up being laborers, ditch diggers, and railroad track men. Many were talented brick layers and cement men. I understand that it was mostly the talented hands of the Italian immigrants that did the beautiful work on Yankee Stadium.

—From *Life in Boonton, USA,* by Joe Marcello

I was told when I came to Boonton, "Never talk about anybody. They're all related." I taught 46 years and I started in 1928. I came from college for an interview to be a kindergarten teacher. My father didn't want me to come to flat New Jersey. "You won't like it," he said. "Don't go." I came anyway. I wore a black satin dress to look older because I looked about 16. I was 21.

I stayed all night in Philadelphia. Then, in the morning when I got to Newark, I found the bus to Boonton. On the bus I asked a lady if we were close to Boonton. "I don't know," she said huffily. I thought I'm not going to like it. Pennsylvania people are so friendly. I'm not going to stay.

We finally got to Boonton and I saw the reservoir. "Oh," I said, "How nice. They have a big lake here." The bus came up Main Street where the Charter Bank was. I got off and there were a lot of men—fellas, sitting around. They started whistling at me. [Laughs.] And I knew I wasn't going to stay in this town.

Anyway, I called and made an appointment with the superintendent of schools, Mr. Mann. When we met he said, "Well, Mrs. Thornton," that was my maiden name at the

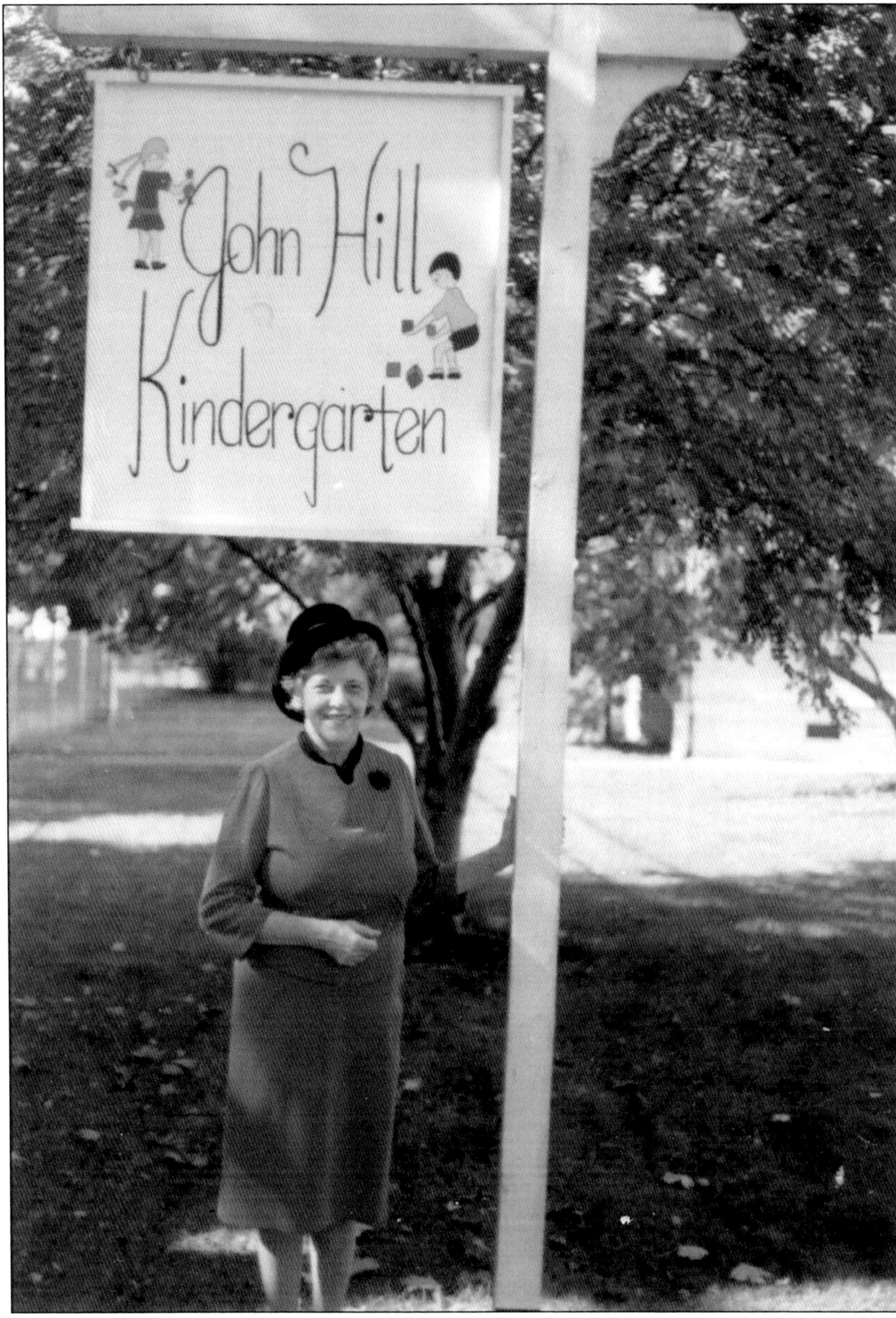

Pat Fowler in 1970.

time, "First of all, do you play the piano? I just fired the kindergarten teacher here because she couldn't play the piano." "Well," I said, "I had eight years of music." He said, "You're hired." [Laughs.]

That was September 1928. He said the salary was 1,500 a year. Pennsylvania was paying their teachers 800. So I was very elated to know that I had a kindergarten job in New Jersey. That was one year before the Depression. So he took me to this very old building which is now the mosque. It used to be the Jewish Temple over here in Harrison School. "Now," he said, "Remember, you won't be here long, maybe a year or so, and you'll be going to one of the prettiest kindergartens in the state of New Jersey," which it was. They were building the John Hill School at the time.

We lived in Mama Teague's Rooming House. She took in only teachers. It was on the corner of Old Boonton Road and Monroe Street. We had all our meals where the Reservoir Tavern is now. There were no cars in those days, and we'd walk there every day. I had a few days off, and my friend was being taken to New York by Bill Scerbo, the father of Al Scerbo, the County Clerk and Freeholder, who was going to the automobile show in New York to buy a new car.

I was so thrilled to see New York. They told me, "Don't look up. They'll know you're from the country." After the automobile show he took us to a place to eat, which we thought must have been Mama Leone's. All I can remember was that I was so impressed. I thought it was a private dining room and there were these velvet, high-backed chairs. Bill Scerbo said, "Now, Mrs. Thornton, what are you going to eat?" And I said, "Chicken." "Chicken," he said. "You can't have chicken in a place like this." I said, "Chicken." And I had chicken.

From the first day of school I loved the little ones. I still love teaching. This man I was engaged to was from Langhorn, Pennsylvania. By Christmas he had already given me a ring. He came from quite a wealthy family. But I wasn't even thinking of getting married. Maybe in 5 years, or 10. But I think his family wanted him to get married. He was a golfer and I think they thought he was going into professional golfing, and they wanted him

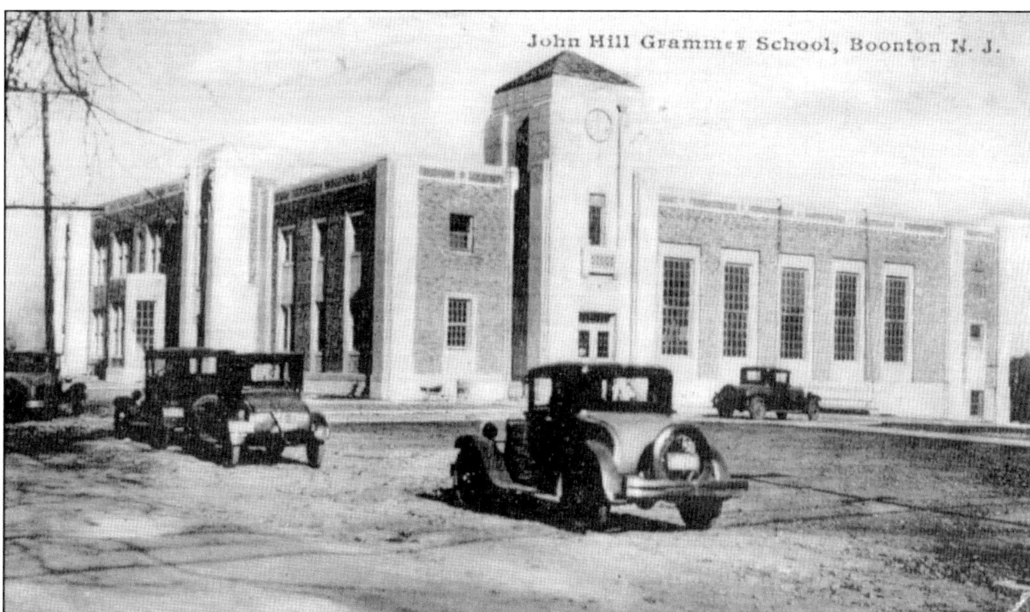

The John Hill Grammar School.

settling down. And I thought I was going to be a golf widow, and I wanted to teach.

So we decided to break off and I told him to come for his ring. I can still see him coming over, parking his car in front of my school and walking up to the entrance. I got the ring out of my pocketbook. And while my children were building with blocks I gave him back his ring in the cloak room.

That was in 1929 and in [19]32 I did get married. My husband died in [19]66, and not having any children I kept on teaching. And I'm still here in Boonton 72 years after I arrived here.

I keep busy. I play bridge four days a week, and I still visit Tally Ho Nursing Home. They're all leaving me, but I'm finding younger friends. I didn't have any children of my own, and I don't have any relatives except second and third cousins. My brother died at 59. My mother died at 69. My dad was 85, and his great uncle was 105. So I'm aiming for that.

What I'm doing now is sorting everything out. At 93 I want to file things so that the only family I have will have less to do. Wherever I go I meet my old students and get kisses. I love it. I meet parents and grandparents I taught. Which thrills me. My oldest student is 78. I had over 2,500 children.

—Pat Fowler

Mrs. Fowler was my kindergarten teacher. She was probably the prettiest teacher in John Hill. And fabulous as a teacher. She cared about all her kids. And she remembers everyone of us today. It's uncanny how she does. I'm 62 and to this day she still calls me "her little boy."

—Anthony Bucco

Chapter Two
The Past

Lenni Lenapes, or the Delaware Native Americans, fished in untamed rivers and hunted in a wild and wooded northwestern New Jersey hundreds of years ago. Their villages were small, their farms cultivated, their orchards fruitful. Occasionally a white trader, strange in this land, would buy their furs. Probably their settlements nearest Boonton were Pompton Plains and Rockaway Valley.

—From *A History of Morris County, New Jersey*

The Lenni Lenape occupied what is now New Jersey, and many were split into numerous small tribes, to which the many beautiful Indian names in New Jersey testify. At the date of my story there were not a great many Indians in New Jersey, the most numerous tribe living at Lake Hopatcong. Nearly all of them had sold their lands to the white settlers, and moved west or north. In a few years thereafter the Indians of New Jersey were merely a tradition. This seems a sad fact, as from the first settlement in the colony at Elizabeth Port, in the year 1665, until the Revolutionary War, when some of the chiefs were induced by Brandt, the Mohawk, to espouse the side of the king, the whites and Indians had lived in entire peace and amity.

—From *Scouts of '76*, by Charles E. Willis

About 1700, the Indians sold this territory to the proprietors of West New Jersey and migrated to Pennsylvania and Ohio. The earliest account we have of the extinguishment of the Indian title to the land upon which Boonton now stands extends back about two hundred years. A short time before the news of the grant made by Charles Second to the Duke of York reached here a number of companies had been organized for the purpose of purchasing lands of the Indians, with a view of establishing new settlements. On the 28th of October, 1664, John Bailey, Daniel Denton and Luke Watson, of Jamaica, on Long Island, purchased of certain Indian chiefs of Staten Island, large tracts of wild lands in East Jersey. These tracts were four in number, and were subsequently known as the Elizabeth, the Mountain, the Horse Neck and the Van Gison. These four tracts were estimated to contain about 400,000 acres, and embraced most of the lands within the present limits of Essex and Morris counties.

The consideration given the Indians for these immense tracts of land was thirty-six pounds fourteen shillings sterling, payable in Indian trinkets at four times their real value, being less than half a mill an acre, and less than an ordinary building lot in Boonton at the present day. (1867.)

Before they left they showed their white companions the strange outcroppings of black rock that they regarded as an oddity to the area. The whites recognized this as iron ore.

—From *The Boonton Years 1867 to 1967*, compiled for the Boonton Centennial Committee

From the point of beginning I have chosen the early 1820's. This period seems to be the transition point of Old Boonton, now covered by the Jersey City reservoir, and present Boonton as it is located today. There may be cause to wonder why the site was selected in the first place, on the side of a hill or mountain as some chose to call it, but we will learn that it was done of necessity rather than choice, for the idea of selecting an ideal choice for a community, certainly never occurred to those responsible.

A major problem of the day was the shortage of fuel. A large number of forges and furnaces that dated back to the early colonial days were now idle and had fallen into a state of disuse, not because of a lack of demand for the product of these establishments, or the availability of the iron ore that abounded in the hills beyond Boonton, but because of the shortage of fuel that was used in the processing of the iron in all of its varied forms.

The fuel of this period was charcoal, and the charcoal was produced by felling trees and cutting them up into suitable lengths to be piled and covered with sod and earth, then to be fired up to burn very slowly in such a manner as to produce a fuel of high carbon content and the ability to produce sufficient heat to melt the iron from the stone. These charcoal pits can still be detected back in the hills as large depressions in the earth, the black soil evidencing the product manufactured there. The charcoal was then transported in large wagons made for the purpose to the manufactories and there consumed, hundreds of bushels used for such "heat" of the furnace.

The fuel situation was a serious problem. The wooded tracts nearby were fast reaching the point of depletion and it meant that fuel would have to come from sources much farther away. This brought about thoughts of a new means of transportation.

The first iron refining forge of record was established by Obidiah Baldwin on the Rockaway River, about a mile and a half downstream from the center of the present town.

The settlement of workmen and their families became the village of "Boone Towne" in honor of the colonial governor, Thomas Boone, in 1761.

The foundry operated illegally, disguised as a mill because the British outlawed the processing of iron by the colonists. Despite this, the forge did a thriving business. During the American Revolution the iron works expanded tremendously. Short supply of manpower attracted Irish and German immigrants to the area. John Jacob Faesch, a Swiss immigrant, one of the most celebrated ironmasters of the country, masterminded the operation for its owner, Mr. David Ogden.

Closely guarded during the war to prevent destruction by the British troops and Tories, the people lived in an armed camp. A quartermaster's post was established there shortly after the beginning of hostilities.

—From *A History of Morris County, New Jersey*

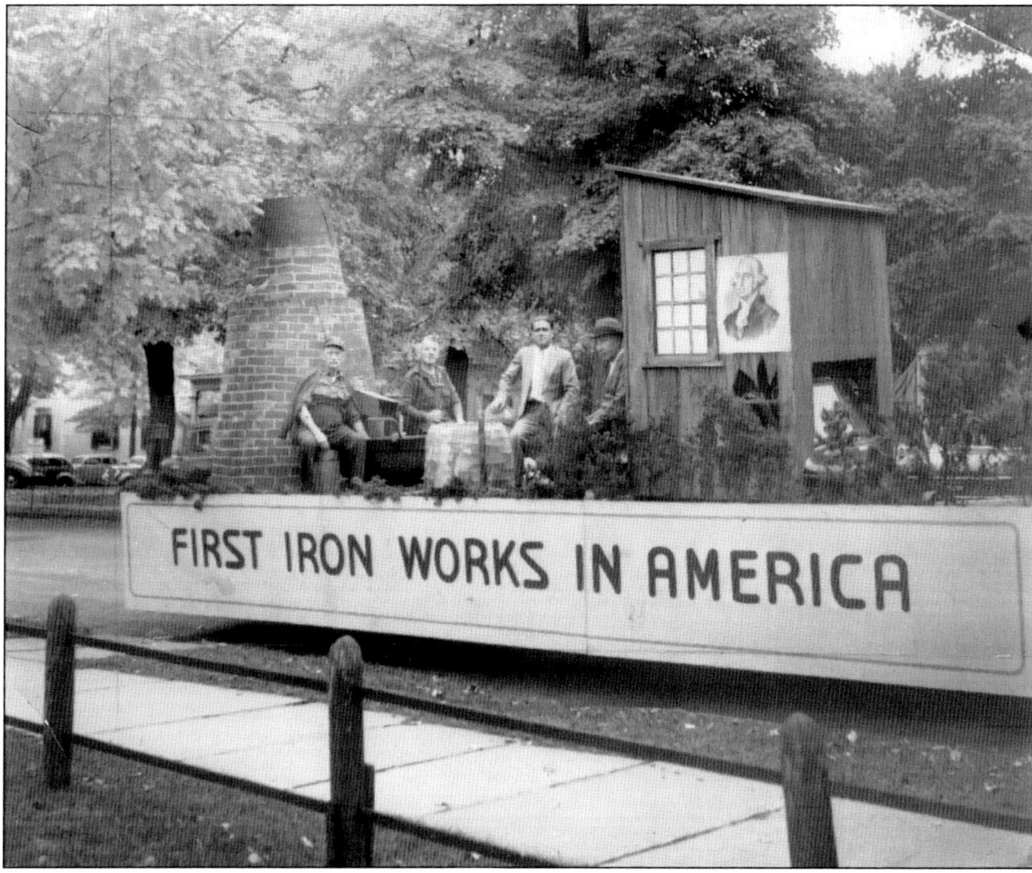

A model of the first ironworks, at the centennial parade.

Nail factories were illegal to have in this country. England just wanted to make the ore that was mined in this country and bring it over there and make the nails themselves and send it back here. Typical colonialism. And a fellow had a nail factory, I think it was Ogden or Faesch, just outside of Boonton.

Nail factories were illegal. And the governor general, who represented England and also happened to be Benjamin Franklin's son, William, had to go around and make occasional inspections, to see that there were no nail factories around. He came by and the owner greeted him very warmly and said, "I'm so glad to see you. I understand you're quite an expert on wines. I just got in a case of wine. I suspect it's tainted and I'd rely on you to give me a good opinion on it." So he brought Franklin down to sample the wines. I guess they spent a good weekend there. [Laughs.] And by the time Franklin left they were in pretty good shape and never got around to inspecting the slitting mill. It was the same thing as Prohibition, when they had a still back in the woods.

In those days nails were a precious commodity. That's why there are so few houses from the [time of the American] Revolution. Nails were a precious commodity. They used to burn down houses to get the nails. They had to build new houses with the nails from the houses they burned down.

—Jim Monaghan

Boonton was then (1830) one of the wildest, rockiest, briarest and most romantic places that the mind of man could imagine and could a man have been foolhardy enough to have prophesied that it would ever become the place that it is even now (1867) he would have been pronounced a lunatic of the most incurable kind, and hurried off to a madhouse with all possible dispatch. . . .

But few of you, I presume, are even acquainted with the gentleman to whose genius and exertions this pleasant and prosperous little village is indebted for its existence; for in this go-ahead age of bustle and strife, but few give themselves the trouble to trace out the laws and affinities that join cause and effect.

In the year 1821 George P. M'Cullock, Esq., a prominent citizen of Morristown, was the man who conceived the bold and original design of constructing the Morris canal. The plausibility of achieving this great work manifested itself to his far-seeing vision, while himself and a party of gentlemen were enjoying a fishing excursion at Hopatcong Lake, more generally known as Brooklyn Pond.

—From *Lyon's Historical Discourse on Boonton*

Although the Morris Canal was built primarily to develop the Pennsylvania anthracite coal trade, it was hoped that a canal routed through the Highlands would also revitalize the New Jersey iron industry. The stories of the canal and the iron business are inextricably intertwined.

. . . When New York's Erie Canal was completed in 1825, it was immediately a huge success. Canal fever swept the coastal states as they competed for access to the rich new western lands. Vast deposits of hard coal had been discovered in eastern Pennsylvania and canals were already planned to bring the new fuel to Philadelphia. New York was becoming the nation's largest port and, thus, couldn't afford to be left out of a major market. A canal across New Jersey was needed, but a route through the Highlands was not a logical choice.

It was George Macculloch, a businessman from Morristown, who realized that, by using the water of Lake Hopatcong, it might be possible to connect the drainage of the Rockaway River on the east with that of the Musconetcong River on the west to build a canal through the heart of New Jersey's iron-producing region. Macculloch counted on the forgemen and ironmasters of Morris County to be among his chief supporters. On December 31, 1824,

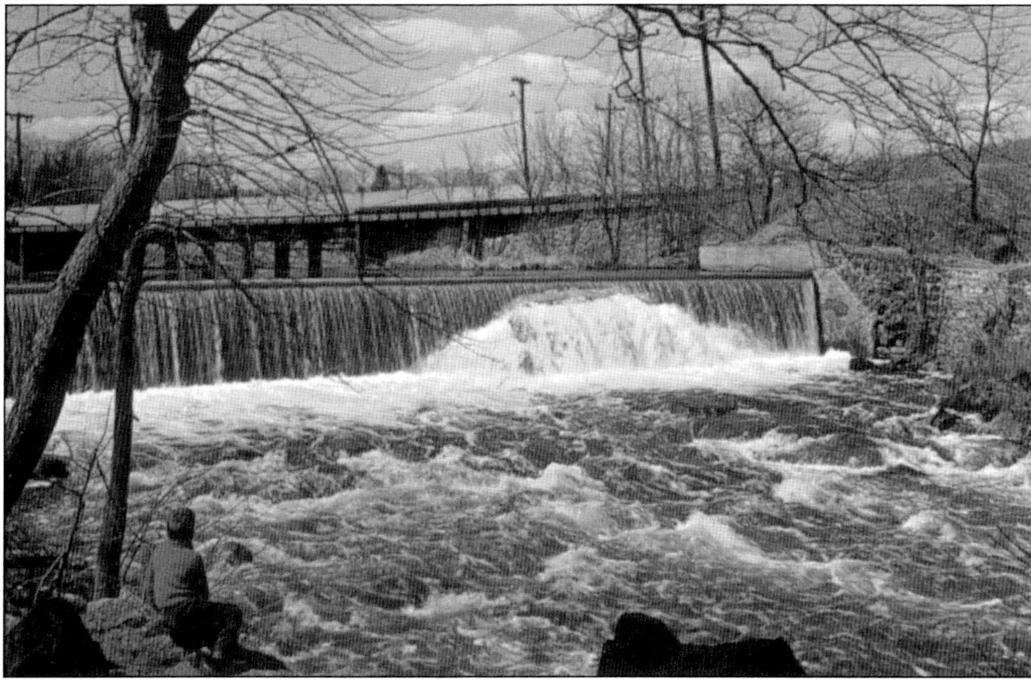

The dam and falls at West Main Street.

the New Jersey Legislature granted a charter to the Morris Canal and Banking Company.

. . . Unlike Montville, the town of Boonton did not exist where it does today before the coming of the Morris Canal. The original town was located a mile to the south along a section of the Rockaway River that is now submerged by the Jersey City Reservoir. In the mid-1740's, David Ogden of Newark erected a forge at what came to be known as Old Boonton. Later, his son, Samuel, took over the business and, in 1770, erected a slitting mill. With energy and skill as an ironmaster, Samuel built the village into a successful iron-making community. In 1784 he leased the works to John Jacob Faesch, the famous ironmaster from Mount Hope. Together they rebuilt the old forge and expanded the operation. The works operated under Faesch's management until his death in 1799. His sons took charge, but their inexperience and a downturn in the market proved fatal to the business. The property had to be sold to pay creditors.

William Scott, a local forge owner, purchased the Old Boonton Tract, including much of the land on which the present town of Boonton now stands. In 1822 he built a road through the property to his forge and gristmill at Powerville. When the Morris Canal and Banking Company planned the route of their canal through the Boonton area, they obtained land from Scott and also the right to dam the Rockaway River above the Boonton Falls. In return, Scott received the right to use the canal as a raceway to carry water to any mill sites that might be built in the ravine below the falls, as long as the water was eventually returned to the canal. Not wishing to develop the property himself, Scott sold 200 acres and the water rights to David Wetmore, an iron merchant from New York who, together with other investors, formed the New Jersey Iron Company.

In 1830 when the Eastern Division of the canal was opened between Newark and Dover, the iron company had already started construction. Puddling furnaces and a rolling mill were installed and, by 1831 when the canal was completed, wrought iron for sheets, hoops and bars was being produced.

As the years passed, the Boonton Ironworks continued to expand. In 1833 a charcoal iron furnace was built and, in 1848, an iron furnace fueled by anthracite coal was added, the second one built in the state. This put the ironworks on the cutting edge of technology. In the same year, a nail factory was built and, in 1868, a second anthracite furnace was constructed. Eventually the manufacturing area stretched from the canal to the river, with 150 nail machines producing 200,000 kegs of nails a year. The ironworks employed as many as 500 workers at a monthly payroll as high as $30,000.

The exclusive relationship between the canal and the ironworks continued until 1864 when a branch line of the Morris and Essex Railroad was built connecting Boonton to the main line at Denville. The prosperity of the ironworks continued until the Panic of 1873 closed the works. Under new management, work was resumed, but in 1880 the Boonton Ironworks closed for the last time.

Finally, in 1903 a disastrous fire ravaged the site, destroying most of the buildings and bringing to a close an important chapter in Boonton's history.

—From *Guide to the Morris Canal in Morris County,* by Joseph J. Macasek

Now it is quite certain and plain to be seen that, had there been no Morris canal, there would have been no iron works located here by the New Jersey Iron Company, and if these works had never been established here the ground upon which Boonton now stands would, in all human probability, have still remained in its old primeval state. Hence it will have at once been seen that Mr. M'Cullock's far-seeing vision was the indirect cause of the first settlement of this place. His pleasure-seeking fishing excursion to Brooklyn Pond was the cause, and the beautiful and thriving village of Boonton is the effect.

My own personal recollections of Boonton extend back almost twenty-eight years. I resided here most of the time during the years 1832–'33 and '34; but the Boonton of those days was a very small and insignificant affair, indeed, as compared with the Boonton of the present day.

In entering the place from any direction at that time you could not see any village at all—nothing but rocks and trees, and these were neither "few nor far between." The Boonton of 1832 consisted of the iron works, two stores, and about twenty small dwelling-houses, all of which were located under the hill, in what is now known as Plane street.

The inhabitants numbered about 300, all told, not more than ten of whom were natives of New Jersey. The whole village, with the exception of one store and two or three dwelling-houses, belonged exclusively to the company.

Excluding the old road (already mentioned), there was no public thoroughfare through the place except by the road *under the hill,* and he that undertook to drive a team in any other direction did so at the risk of life and limb, both to himself and animals. . . .

At that time most of the iron works were carried on under the same roof. They consisted of a rolling mill, a number of puddling and heating furnaces, an old-fashioned trip-hammer, a slitting machine and a small foundry. They were principally engaged in the manufacture of sheet, hoop and bar iron. . . . There was also a refinery, which stood on the bank of the river. . . . At that time the only public conveyance between this place and New York was by stage, three times a week . . . All our mail matter had to be obtained from the post office at Parsippany, 3½ miles distant, which had a tri-weekly mail.

The company used to dispatch a wagon to meet each mail, with orders to bring over the letters and papers for this place to their store, from whence they were delivered to their owners when called for.

—From *Lyon's Historical Discourse on Boonton*

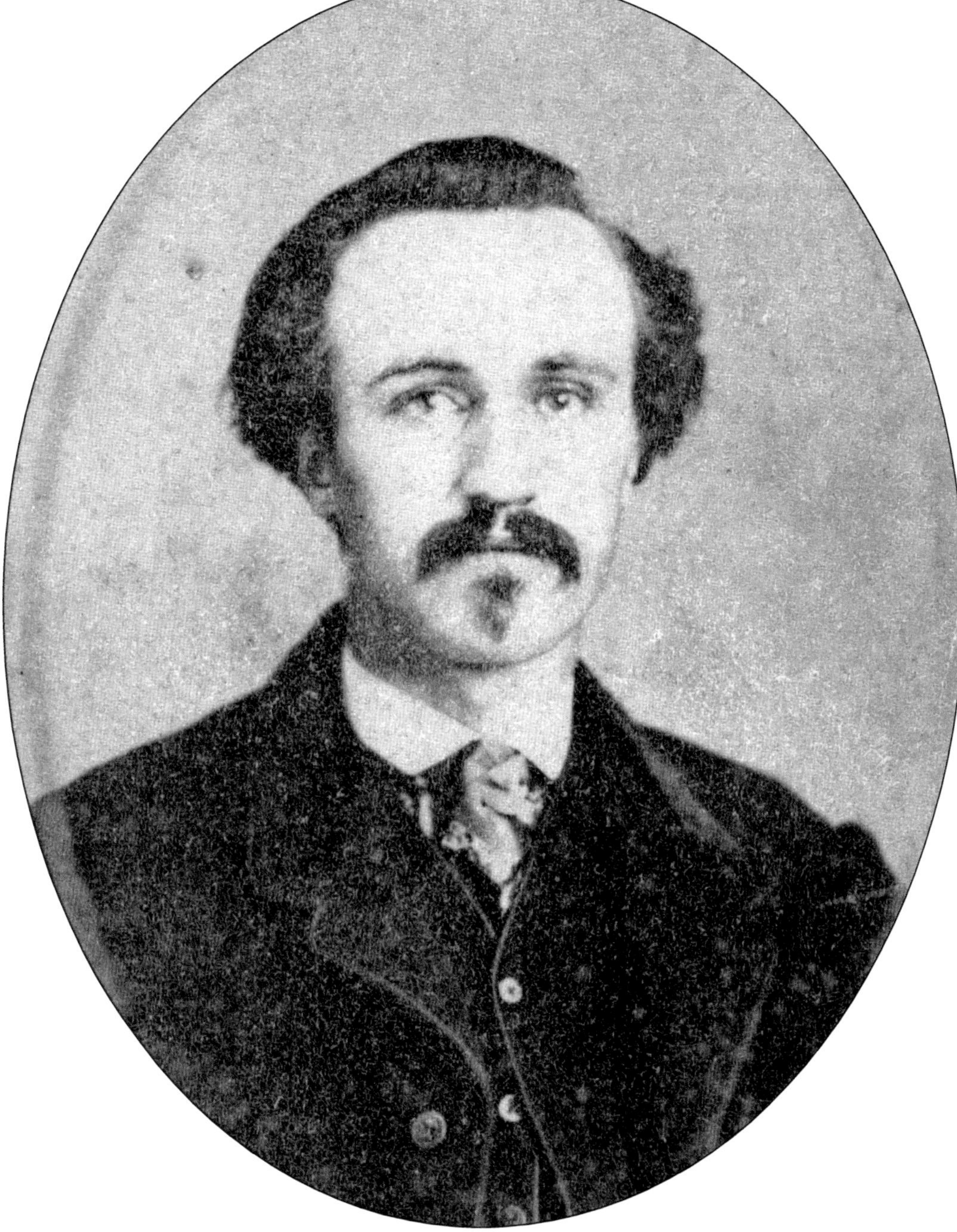

Dr. John Grimes, noted abolitionist.

Excerpts from
The Boonton Years 1867 to 1967,
compiled for the Boonton Centennial Committee:

Boonton's Booming
In 1860, the population of Boonton was 2,230, made up of 419 families who lived in 326 dwellings. . . . The oldest person living in Boonton was 85 years old. . . . Real estate was valued at $79,725 and the value of personal goods was $175,700. . . . Even then, there were more people than cows, which numbered 1,219.

One of the outstanding figures of the pre-Civil War period in Boonton was Dr. John Grimes. He was dedicated to the cause of abolition and was a vital link in the underground railroad chain which spirited about 40,000 slaves through New Jersey northward to freedom. He was not always a popular man, but seemed to prefer the dignity of standing on his ideals and principles to the approbation of his fellowmen. He was a vegetarian and attempted to encourage others to this diet by sponsoring vegetarian dinners and meetings at Liberty Hall, which he built about 1844 on Main Street, near the corner of Liberty Street. . . . It seemed that he was on the unpopular side of nearly every public issue—politics, religion, temperance and diet. . . . He served as secretary in the Anti-Slavery Society of the state and published Boonton's first newspaper. . . . On April 19, the First Congregational Society of Boonton was incorporated. Dr. John Grimes, George W. Esten, John Maxfield, James S. Norris and Daniel C. Norris were named in the Society. . . . Among those who helped in the [struggle] were William G. Lathrop, John Hill, Thomas Willis, Philip Wootton, George Ely, Charles B. Norris, Frederick Stone, James Grimes, George Coates, Nathan Hopkins and his son Charles F. Hopkins.

A young nephew of the doctor's, Josiah Quincy Grimes, came to work for his uncle in 1861. The lad kept a diary which reveals some homely facts of life in Boonton 100 years ago. He writes:

> Uncle John wants me . . . to keep the drug shop and sometimes put out the horse, split some wood, etc., for the consideration of five dollars per month. . . . Took a walk about the canal this morning, saw them cast at the blast furnace. . . . At night I went to see the blast furnace, and took a ride on the plane. . . . Sold some arsenic to a woman this afternoon, went swimming with Symon . . . in the canal. . . . In the afternoon a man came in and wanted to be bled, so Uncle stuck him in the arm and I held a basin to catch the blood. When it got about one-sixth full Uncle stopt the operation and I emptied the basin in the street.

The Civil War: 1861–1865
Fire was opened by General Beauregard at 4 A.M., Friday, the 12th, from seven batteries . . . and at 12:55 P.M Saturday, the American Flag was lowered . . . Fort Sumter evacuated by Major Anderson.

—From the *Jerseyman*, April 12, 1861

The fire of heroism burns brightly in Boonton. The Captain of the military company there had aroused "Old Pequannoc," and at least two hundred of as hardy, stalwart men as ever dashed a bayonet charge, could be raised in a week's time. They were hungering and thirsting after a chance to meet our aristocratic foes. Shall they not have it? The uniformed company is a splendid one, and what a mine of true gold is in the spirit and muscle of the undrilled athletes of that village.

The Nail Factory now presents an animated appearance. Some two hundred of those savage iron-eating machines have small flags of the stars and stripes pattern affixed to their moving parts, as they keep bobbing up and down in ceaseless movement, help no doubt to fan the flame of love for Country, and for home and honor.

—From the *Paterson Guardian*, April 12, 1861

Proclamation by the Governor, State of New Jersey

I do, therefore, recommend that all volunteer companies now forming throughout the State and all other persons of the proper age disposed to do so, organize themselves as volunteer companies, according to the act of the Legislature of 1860, as promptly as may be, so that there may be a large body of effective militia in the State, ready for any call that may be made upon them.

All volunteer companies thus organized will be armed by the State, with the provisions of the aforesaid act, as soon as proper arms can be obtained.

By the Governor,
Charles S. Olden
W.S. Johnson, Secretary of State
Dated Trenton, May 2, 1861

Charles F. Hopkins was a hard man to kill. Leg wounds, a head wound, starvation, scurvy, typhoid and gangrene couldn't finish off the hardy Civil War veteran from Boonton who lived to the age of 92.

Hopkins' heroics earned him a Medal of Honor, making him the only Boonton native to earn the nation's highest military honor.

The Civil War carried Hopkins far from Boonton and into perils a less determined man would not have survived.

Twice Hopkins was left for dead, once from a head wound after carrying a wounded comrade-in-arms from the battlefield.

The second time was after the liberation of a Confederate prison camp.

A Civil War Soldier

On February 27, 1865, at the Confederate prison camp in Florence, S.C., the last few hundred Union prisoners were marched to the nearby railroad to await transportation to freedom. Only 24 were left behind, those being considered hopelessly ill, defeated by starvation, disease and despair.

But one of those 24 was indomitable. Refusing to surrender to death, Cpl. Charles F. Hopkins of Boonton crawled from the vermin infested hospital shed and dragged his gangrenous legs across the frozen ground toward the tracks.

Thus began the homeward journey of this courageous soldier who had seen the war through from the first disastrous battle of Bull Run to the hell hole that was Andersonville prison in Georgia, a place of slow execution for 13,700 Union troops.

Along the way Charles Hopkins received several wounds, a strengthening of his belief in freedom, and the Congressional Medal of Honor.

A member of Boonton's National Guard Company G at the outbreak of the war, Charles was too impatient to await his unit's induction.

—From *The Boonton Years 1867 to 1967*, compiled for the Boonton Centennial Committee

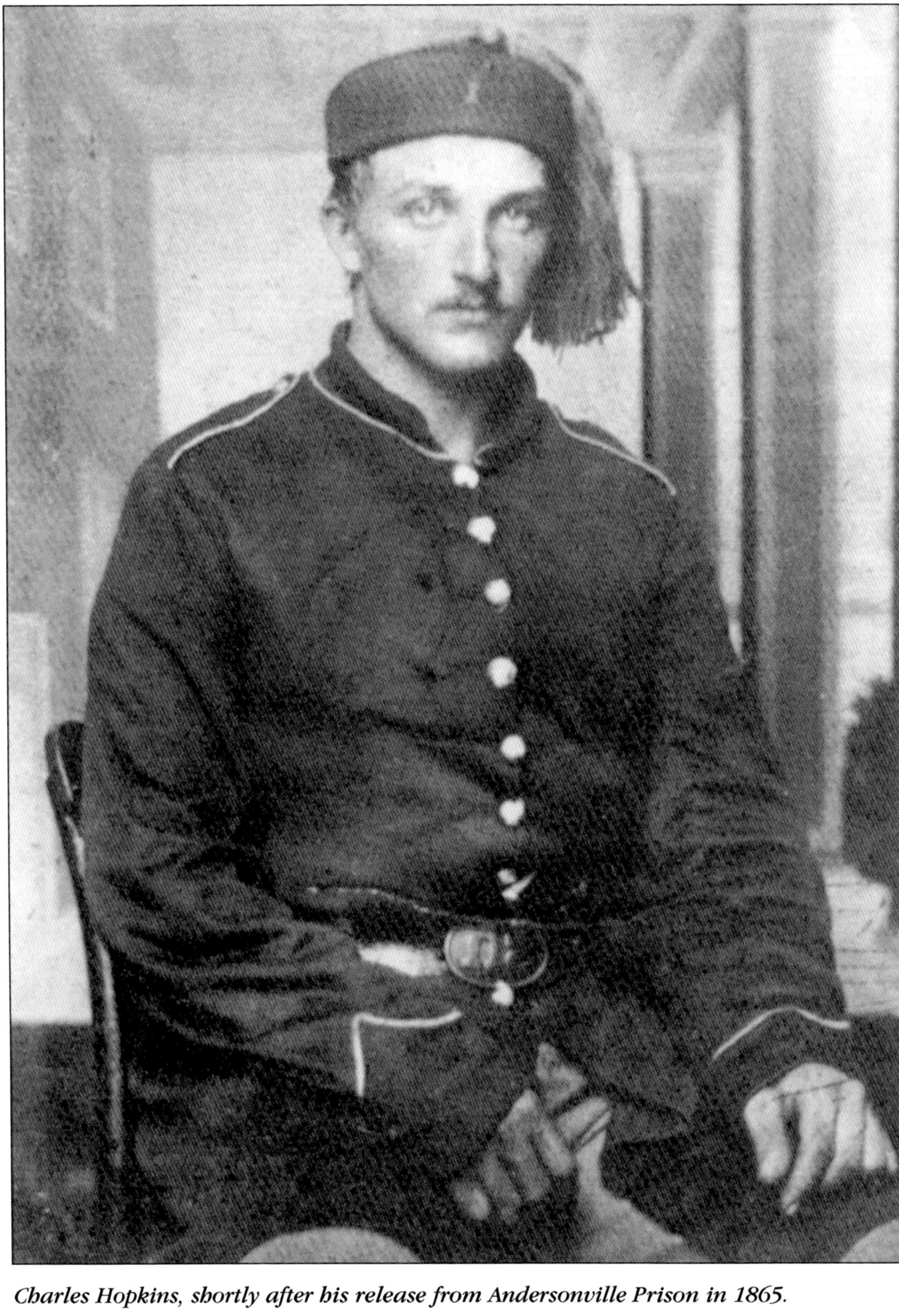

Charles Hopkins, shortly after his release from Andersonville Prison in 1865.

Quite unwilling to await the seemingly slow process (though found sufficiently swift a few months later) of offering our services and being accepted as a Company; with more patriotic fervor than good sense, on the 3rd of May, 1861, without due parental notice and sanction, I startled the family at the breakfast table (minus the head of the family, who left early to be absent the whole day) with, "Ellen, I want a clean shirt. I am going away!" Ellen, who was my stepmother, and a good one, and her two daughters, who were as sisters, were the only persons present, the one whom I did not wish to consult on the question, my father, was absent as before stated. I had chosen this auspicious time, in order to avoid a collision that might prove all my nicely laid plans abortive. In reply to my good stepmother's question, "Charlie, where are you going?" "To war!" came the prompt reply, and I imagine there may have been some bombast in the tone, for I was chuck full of enthusiasm to go to war. With the tears and pleading of Mother and her daughters, I had to brace up pretty firmly—and won. The bundle was neatly wrapped, and many other things urged upon me, but I was no pack horse then, no matter how much of a pack mule I was later on. I pleaded stage time which was close at hand as I could hear the rumbling of Jake Meslar's thorough-brace, old rocking stage. Hastily embracing and kissing all good-bye, not forgetting to leave a good-bye to the absent father, the stage passed the door—and I became an unexpected passenger.

I sprang on the boot at the rear of the old Ark, crawled to the roof and surprised Old Jake, who gave me a dark scowl as I paid him the usual thirty cents for an uncomfortable ride to Denville. . . . We reached our goal, New York City, and visited the Battery, intending to enlist in the Second Militia Regiment of New York, from which some eight hundred had already gone forward to Washington and the front. When about to enlist, we learned from the newspaper that there had been a mutiny among them at Washington, and thereupon we stoutly refused to become that kind of a patriot.

We searched from one headquarters to another, until finally, in disgust, we crossed the river to my native State. At Hoboken, I was "taken in" in right smart order, along with a Yankee, whose acquaintance I had made at the Battery, by his proffer to me to share his umbrella. He hailed from the land of Wooden Nutmegs, and this friendship was to ripen into a life long comradeship, both in the service and to this hour—with seventy-eight years to my credit, and eighty-five to his. We were sent to Trenton, New Jersey, on the day following our visit to Hoboken, and became members of Company I, 1st New Jersey Volunteers.

—From *The Andersonville Diary and Memoirs of Charles Hopkins*

In May of 1864, with Grant in charge and Lee falling back toward Richmond in a series of bloody engagements, the two armies found themselves in a forested stretch of Virginia called the Wilderness.

Twice wounded, the Boonton soldier was ordered to the rear by his captain but refused. "I contended that to go to the rear was as dangerous as to remain with the company and remain I did."

With only three days left in his enlistment he was captured and began his long trip southward to "that abode of misery, starvation and death"—Andersonville, Ga.

—From *The Boonton Years 1867 to 1967*, compiled for
the Boonton Centennial Committee

Inside the camp death stalked on every hand. The death at hands of the guard, though murder in cold blood, was merciful beside the systematic, studied, absolute murder inside, by slow death, inch by inch!

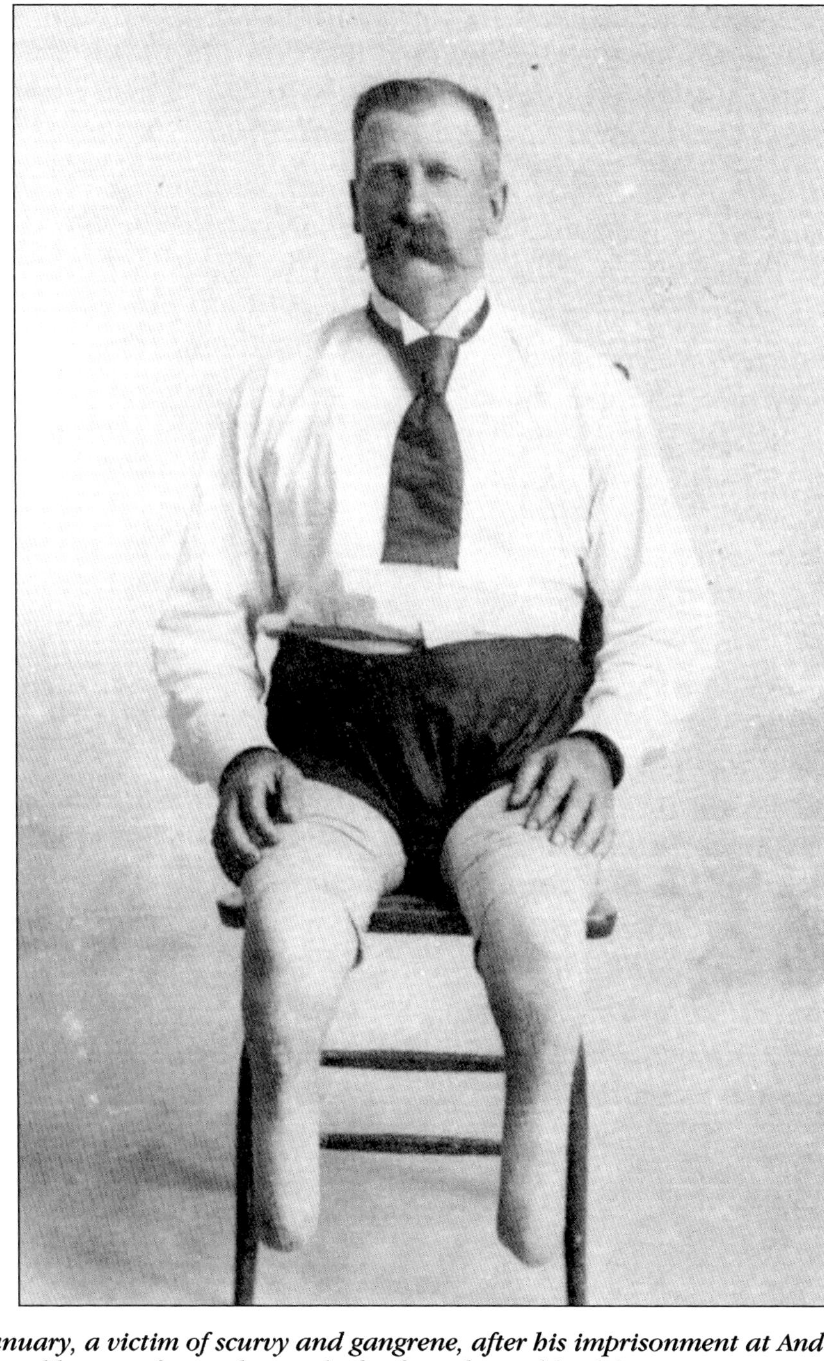

John January, a victim of scurvy and gangrene, after his imprisonment at Andersonville, amputated his own feet with a pocketknife and saved his life.

. . . I have known over 3000 men to wait in line to get water, and the line was added to as fast as reduced, from daylight to dark . . . men taking turn of duty with men of their Mess, in order to hold their place in line, as no man could stand it alone, even if in the "pink" of physical condition; the heat of the sun, blistering him, or the drenching rains soaking him, not a breath of fresh air, and we had no covering but Heaven's canopy. Air-loaded with unbearable, fever-laden stench from the poison sink of putrid mud and water. . . . We could not get away from it—we ate it, drank it and slept in it. . . .

What wonder that men died, or were so miserable as to prefer instant death . . . and so preferring, deliberately stepping within the deadline and looking their willing murderer in the eye, while the shot was sent crashing through the brain that was yet clear. . . . One poor demented comrade, not instantly killed, lay for hours in full view of his comrades—gasping and struggling with death, but no one would go to his rescue for fear of the same kind of death. Men, who at one time, were lion-hearted, brave in battle, shuddered at the sight, and wept like children, and cursed the murderer. This victim was a demented, starved, one-legged veteran who had lost his leg at Chickamauga. . . .

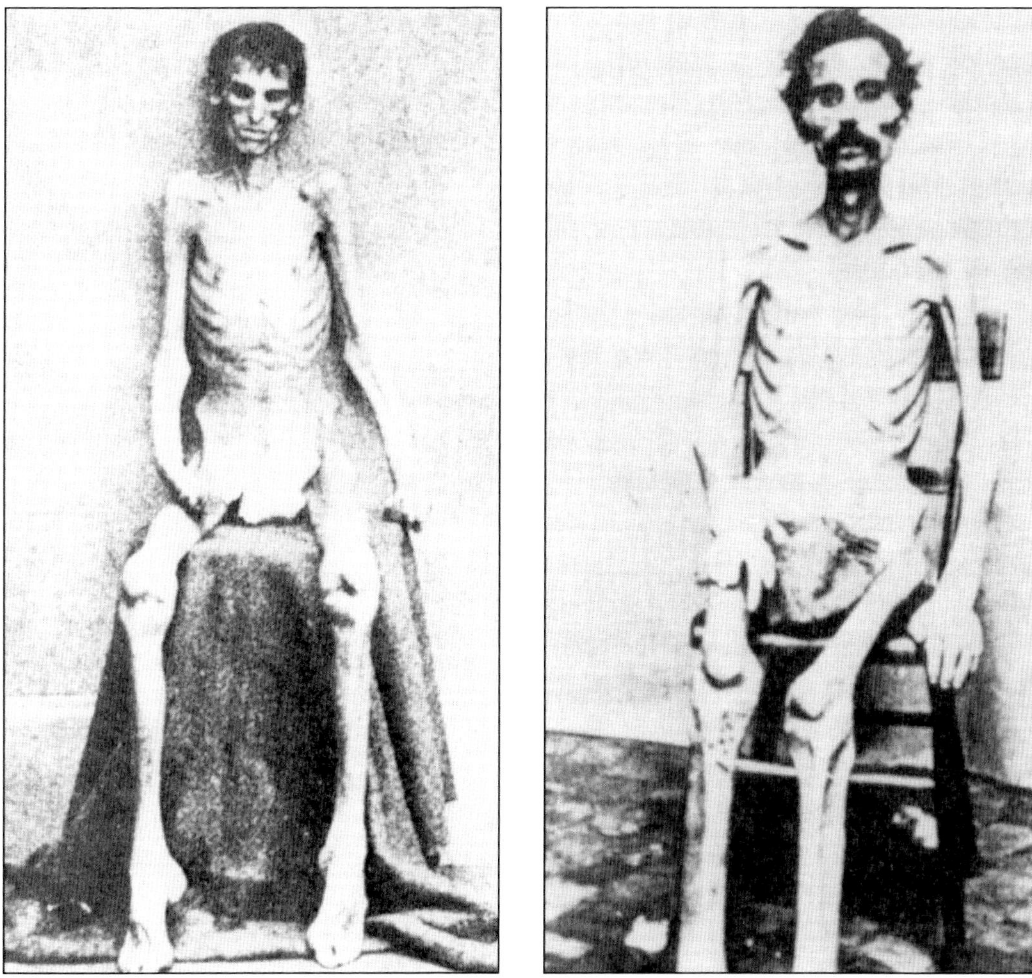

The "living skeletons" of Andersonville. Photographs were taken of the survivors to show the American people what crimes had been committed at Andersonville and Florence Prisons.

Tuesday, July 19, 1864

The nights of July, after sundown, steadily cooled so that before morning it became quite cold for most of us, minus clothes and no covering. In August and September—to the thirteenth—we found ourselves getting up on all fours, gradually stretching out to the rays of the sun, to nearly normal height. Any day now you could see numbers of men wading from knee to waist deep in the liquid, fetid filth of the swampy level—groping with the hope of finding some roots to dry or wood to cook over the half-baked stuff sent in—such was the scarcity of wood inside, with acres and acres of wood about us, only to look at.

Woe to him that had the slightest sore or abrasion of the skin which might come in contact with that polluted mass—gangrenous sores resulted, low fevers of the camp engendered—the horrible sores the contact produced seem incredible to tell of, but the facts were undeniable. Cancer-like, they eat into the little flesh that the victims had, bared the sinews and bond—the poor fellows rotted by inches. Starvation, polluted water, exposure to sun and rain, and cold nights and many of them of a truly sleepless night, brought on fevers that were almost surely fatal—causing delirium of several types.

The cases of insanity were numerous. Men, strong in mentality, heart and hope were in a few short months, yes, often in a few weeks, reduced to imbeciles and maniacs. Today they know you and look upon you as friends and comrades; tomorrow they are peevish, whining, childish creatures, or raving maniacs.

Some would beg for something to eat; others asked for wife, mother, children or other relatives; some, in their delirium were home talking to their friends, enjoying the good eating that Mother set before them—they seemed happy, many forever talking of hunger and a goodly number were furiously wild, and had they been strong they would have been dangerous—not knowing their closest friend, trusting no one, raving and cursing in fearful language. Happily, may I say it, all such died soon, worn out and exhausted by this emotion. . . . The average deaths per day for seven and a half months were eighty-five.

Natural causes, indeed!! There were murders committed by most "unnatural causes" and methods—systematic causes! Orders were issued that all should be vaccinated, and yet in all that den of filth, dirt, starvation, polluted water, vermin, flies, reeking with the filth of the open sinks, and polluted swap mosquitos ever at hand, small pox cut no figure whatever, to October at least. Squads of ninety were ordered up to the gate for their possible death warrant. "Vaccination."

Some were fortunate enough not to "take;" others, the moment they were treated and could turn aside, wiped the vaccine off and cleansed the spot by sucking the blood from it in order that no vaccine virus be left to work its destruction; some evaded it by tricks and lies. The writer did his own "scratching" and covered the wound with mucous from his mouth—which may have been as dangerous had it been left to work its "scurvy" destiny—and bared his arm for inspection, which was no trouble, as my shirt was armless . . . the inspector followed and passed me as "done." By this deception we escaped a death perhaps that hundreds found at the hands of those who had used impure vaccine matter. . . . One of them a black hero of Burnside's Brigade of negroes, had lost a leg and an arm at the Wilderness and had, up to this time, been able to say that he was recovering from both those fearful wounds.

Not satisfied with this dusky man's misfortune and suffering, which were self-evident, the authorities could not forget the "exquisite" pleasure it gave them to inject their "system" of death from "natural causes" into the blood of this man they so grudgingly hated because of his color, and because he was in Uncle Sam's uniform.

That poor fellow died a short month later from this poison that became a part of his wounds and the arm on which he was operated had been amputated half-way between shoulder and elbow and was eaten away as if by cancer, until death came to his relief, at which time the tendons and bone were fully exposed. "Natural causes"—My God!!!!!

What a record [Confederate general John H.] Winder and [commandant of Andersonville Prison, Capt. Henry] Wirz took to Hell with them! They must have surprised the Devil by their heinous crimes, and Satan must have given them the highest rating!

—From *The Andersonville Diary and Memoirs of Charles Hopkins*

A Proclamation by the President of the United States of America
March 30, 1863
Whereas, the Senate of the United State devotedly recognizing the supreme authority and government of Almighty God in all affairs of men of nations, has, by a resolution requested the President to designate and set apart a day for National Prayer and Humiliation, and,

Whereas, it is the duty of nations, as well as men, to own their dependence upon the overruling power of God, to confess their sins and transgressions, in humble sorrow, yet with the assured hope that genuine repentance will lead to mercy and pardon, and to recognize the sublime truths announced in the Holy Scriptures and proven by all history, that those nations only are blessed whose God is the Lord:

And inasmuch as we know that, by His Divine Law, nations like individuals, are subjected to punishment and chastisement in this world, may we not justly fear that the awful calamity of civil war which now so desolates the land, may be but a punishment inflicted upon us for our presumptuous sins, to the needful end of our national reformation as a whole People? We have been the recipients of the choicest bounties of Heaven.

We have been preserved, these many years in peace and prosperity. We have grown in numbers, wealth and power as no other nation has ever grown. But we have forgotten God. We have forgotten the gracious hand which preserved us in peace, and multiplied and enriched and strengthened us: and we have vainly imagined, in the deceitfulness of our hearts, that all these were produced by some superior wisdom of our own. Intoxicated with unbroken success, we have become too self-sufficient to feel the necessity of redeeming and preserving grace, too proud to pray to the God that made us.

It behooves us, then, to humble ourselves before the offended Power, to confess our national sins, and pray for clemency and forgiveness. . . .

—Abraham Lincoln

PEACE THROUGH VICTORY! THE REBELLION CRUSHED
Gen. Lee Surrenders With His Whole Army
Sunday, the 9th of April was made ever memorial in the glorious history of the Nation, by the announcement of the SURRENDER OF GEN. LEE AND HIS WHOLE ARMY.

It is the harbinger of an immediate and glorious Peace, a Peace gloriously won by the grand courage, and unshaken faith in their cause of the splendid Armies of the Potomac and the James, aided by their glory-crowned brethren under Sherman and Sheridan and Thomas and Hancock, and the heroes of the ocean who have kept watch and ward along our coasts from the Delaware to the Rio Grande. It is the end of the Confederacy. . . .

PRESIDENT LINCOLN ASSASSINATED
Attempt to murder Sec'y Seward
The great joy of our victories, so promising in view of peace, has been abruptly broken and supplanted with a sorrow as great, by an event that no true American ever believed possible in this country. President Lincoln has been assassinated by a hand raised in behalf of these traitors, whose quarter of a century of plotting thus receives its appropriate stamp just as their hollow hopes are bursting into ruin.

The time selected was in many repeats opportune for the commission of the terrible act. It had been widely published that the President, and General Grant, with their wives and others, were to be present at Ford's Theatre on Friday evening, April 14th. Mr. Colfax,

Speaker of the House of Representatives, called at the White House in the evening, and Mr. Lincoln remarked that he did not want to go, especially as Mrs. Lincoln was not well, but as General Grant had been obliged to go North, he was unwilling further to disappoint the people. He went, and occupied a box in a tier above the stage, together with his wife, another lady, and an officer of the army. During a momentary hush, while an actor was preparing to enter upon the stage, the report of a pistol was heard, but without exciting suspicion in the unsuspecting audience. But loud screams were heard from Mrs. Lincoln, and at the same instant a man was seen to leap from the box down to the stage, brandishing a large dagger, and shouting "Sic semper tyrannis!" (the motto of the State of Virginia) and "The South is avenged!"

He rushed across the stage, and out of the side door. . . .

—From the *Jerseyman*

On April 11, 1865, just after Robert E. Lee's surrender ended the Civil War, a crowd had gathered to serenade President Abraham Lincoln. Speaking from the White House balcony, he said, "We meet this evening, not in sorrow, but in gladness of heart." He hoped for "a righteous and speedy peace whose joyous expression cannot be restrained."

The address was Lincoln's last. Four days later, he was dead.

—From the *Jerseyman*, April 22, 1865

Boonton's Bound to Go Ahead, by Maudie Fischer

There was in Boonton a man named Isaac S. Lyon. He worked for a time in New York City and returned to the "beautiful and romantic little hillside village" of Boonton. He was a dairyman with the soul of a poet, if not the precise vigilance of a historian.

He fancied himself a historian, nevertheless, and composed a 58-page booklet entitled "Lyon's Historical Discourse on Boonton." Actually, it appears to be a record of several speeches "delivered before the Citizens of Boonton at Washington Hall on the evenings of September 21 and 28 and October 5, 1867 by Isaac S. Lyon, Ex-Cartman."

. . . He urges his fellow townspeople to "invest your greenbacks in Boonton property. Everything was coming up roses for Boonton, Isaac said.

"Yes, the New Yorkers, with their fast horses and long purses, will come. . . . We will then kick poor old sleepy-headed Morristown out of our path and go on our way rejoicing."

Indeed, he rejoiced so ecstatically he had to burst into song. And this he did after his discourses to the public at Washington Hall.

He includes the song in his "history" of Boonton, preceding it with a modest introduction.

"The following homespun song, manufactured expressly for the occasion, was sung by the writer in his exceedingly fascinating style . . . he is pretty strongly impressed with the belief that he is about the only person on the face of the earth who could sing at all: Boonton's Bound to go Ahead!" [A parenthetical note advises: (To be said or sung to any tune that suits it.)]

There are 29 verses to part first and 25 to part second, but here's a sample. Make up your own music.

Soon you'll hear the snorting locomotive
Thundering along the iron road.
Then will come the New York millionaire,
And join us round the festive board—
For Boonton's bound to go ahead!

New Jersey now commands the highway peace
Between the haughty states of York and Penn;

And, if they do not soon their bragging cease,
From crossing our State we'll sure be stopping them—
For Little Jersey's bound to go ahead!

Number Please, by Maudie Fischer

By 1885, anyone could make a phone call in Boonton. The silk mill, operated by the Paterson-based firm of Pelgram and Meyer, had installed a telephone line to its home plant earlier, but until Oct. 29, 1895, the only public phone in town was at the S.S. Lyon general store at the corner of Liberty and Main Streets.

The "Boonton Weekly Bulletin" reports in the Feb. 26, 1885 issue: "The telephone is now in successful operation at S.S. Lyons Store."

In those very early days, to get folks used to the idea of talking into a gol-durn contraption, the Telephone Company held a kind of open house from time to time. They called it "free day" and you could crank 'er up and call anyone at all, for free. You can't beat those rates.

In 1895, however, the rush for service (11 subscribers) led the New York Telephone Company to install the first Boonton switchboard in Mr. Lyon's emporium, with himself as operator while business behind the counter was slow. Among the 3,300 souls comprising Boonton at the time, those who subscribed to this electronic contact with the outside world included John H. Brown, who had the easy to remember Boonton 1 number. The Delaware and Lackawanna Railroad came along with Boonton 2.

For the extremely limited and cumbersome service available, they paid about $42 yearly.

By 1900, there were two kinds of service available. For $50 a year you could make 500 "messages." An additional 10¢ per message was charged beyond that number. An option for $75 allowed unlimited calls within Boonton. The second location of Boonton's switchboard was in the Holmes Library at the corner of Main and Church streets, where Miss Mame Worman was the operator.

—From *The Boonton Years 1867 to 1967*, compiled for the Boonton Centennial Committee

Chapter Three
Working on the Canal

In the year of 1866, A.D., at the age of eleven years, I started my career in life as a boat boy.

When I was told that I would have to make a full hand with my father on the boat, I thought it would be fine and I felt like a full grown man, and was very willing to do my part. I began to get ready for the big adventure. The night before, Mother told me a lot of things which have been my guide through life. Two things I will state she said, "I wish that you would never use tobacco." And then she said, "I want you to promise me that you will never drink any whiskey or beer." All through the 67 years I have kept that promise, and I am glad I did. (And I hope that all the boys and girls who read this will do as I have done) It pays 100 percent and that is a good investment.

The next morning I was off on my first trip on the canal. One thing I would like to say, before I go on is, that as I lay in bed just thinking, I heard Mother say to Father, "Remember, Dan, he is only a child yet." Looking back to that five years so long ago, I know that my father never forgot. He was a wonderful father. Just to state three different incidences, when the nights were long, dark and stormy, and I was plodding along through the storm and mud, above the storm and the wind, I could hear my father sing with his fine baritone voice, "When I Can Read My Title Clear to Mansions in the Skies" and "Other Refuge Have I None." It was more beautiful than I can tell. Another time when we were blown out across the marshes in the Hackensack River, we were out there for two days and nights, and I was very much worried. He would say, "Now, Son, don't be afraid; Our Heavenly Father will take care of us."

And once when we were the last boat in a tow going up the Passaic River, there came up a very hard shower and heavy wind. My father and I stood on the hinge deck of the boat; it was very rough and things looked very bad to me. Father took hold of my hand and I looked up at him. He smiled and I was not afraid. I am mentioning this because in afterlife in meeting the storms that came to me along life's pathways, many times I have taken the great hand of our Father in Heaven, and He had looked down and smiled, and I have had the courage to go on and do my best. . . . Our first trip was through to Jersey City. Everything was new but I got along real good. I was a little worked up when we came to Newark.

I had to leave the boat at the head of the plane at Newark and meet it when it came out from under Mulberry Street. I don't know how far it was, I will say it was quite some over a mile and again Father said 'Don't worry. The mules will get you through all-right.' Good ole mules!

—George Mowder

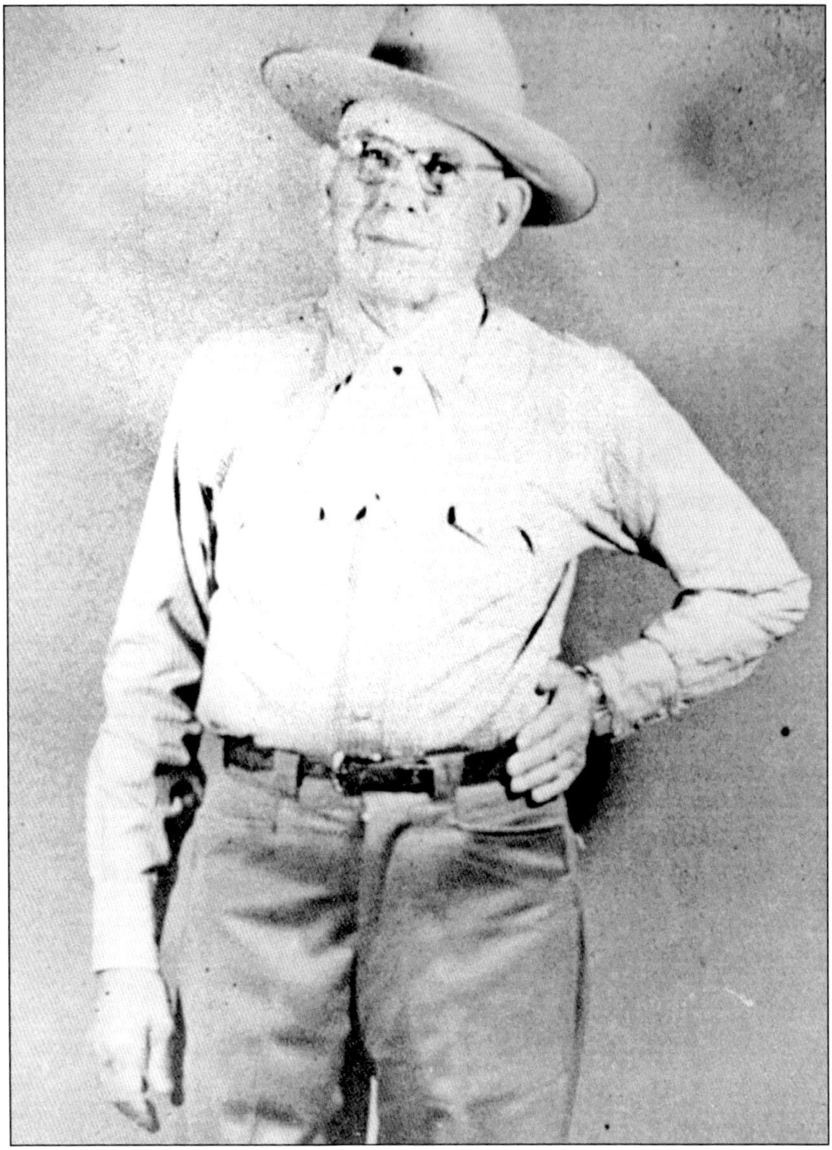

George Mowder, age 67.

(From *Tales the Boatmen Told*)

Faithful mules and horses,
They toiled so hard and long,
Pulling heavy canal boats
While boatboys walked along.

Dan Mowder drove his "Blue Mule"
He'd call to one and all.
Those canallers had their stories,
And some were mighty tall.

Yes, those good old mules are gone now,
But I can hear them even today.
The clump of their shoes on the tow-path,
Their snorts and affectionate bray.

—Famous Morris Canal Mules (of the early 1890s).
(Excerpts from a poem written by Lorraine Willever of Belvidere, New Jersey, from material supplied by Charles Matlock Hummer, a former boatman; from *Tales the Boatmen Told*)

We arrived in Jersey City and it was a great sight for me to see so many things, boats of all kinds, and then looking across the Hudson River into New York City, with its thousands of lights at night. It was wonderful to me.

—George Mowder
(From *Tales the Boatmen Told*)

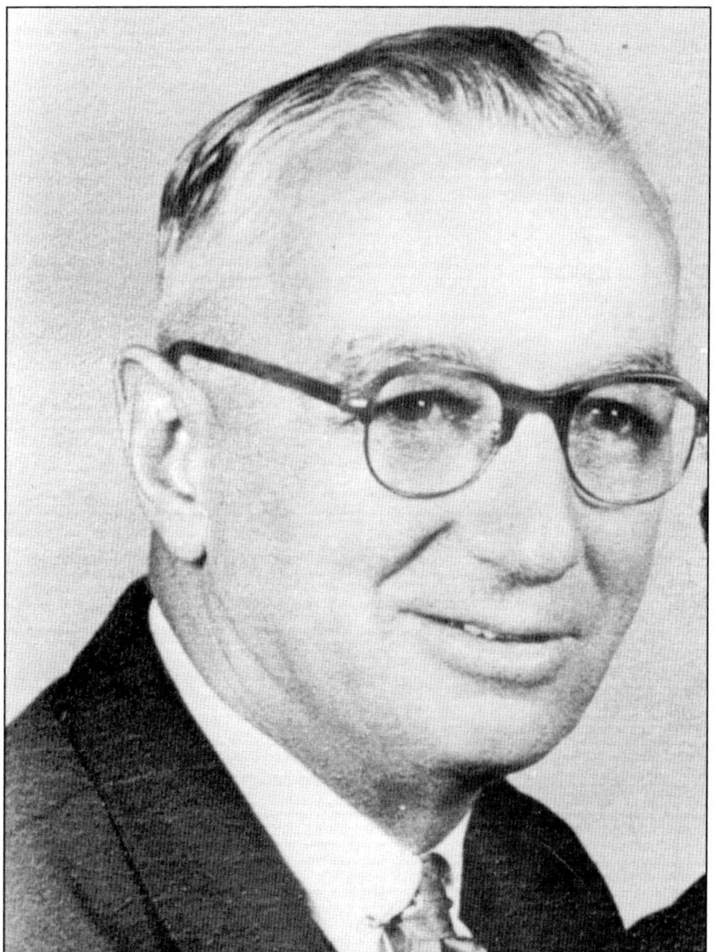

Simon Johnston, canal boat captain.

You didn't have to know anything about reading and writing. All you had to know was which way to take the boat and steer the boat and get it to its destination. We didn't get much. I would say about $50 a trip. . . .

The only time I was afraid was up here one time right at New Village under the bridge up there. I saw something sticking out of the water and when I came to look at it, it was a dead man looking at me. . . . Boy, I was scared. I was just a young fellow. I will never forget that experience. . . . He stoned himself. He drowned himself.

. . . I thought it was a pretty good life. It was a hard life when you stop to look at it now—living on a boat. It was just a little square place where you slept and ate and everything. I slept under the water there all the time practically, and kept my shoes in the dry. It was very cold for us boys. We didn't have shoes to wear. We went bare-footed. . . . And then I came on up (this was later though) and for some reason we were fast or something and we laid there. The level was low, I guess, and we could not go any more. I laid down on the towpath and boy, I woke up and the rats were on me—all over me. . . . We slept on them boats . . . families were raised on that little cabin . . . we didn't have automatic washers . . . bathtubs . . . and no toilet. . . . Think of what them poor boys had to do. When they had to go to the toilet, they had to go under a tree or in the bushes along the canal.

Oh, you rusty old canaller,
You think you're mighty nice.
Standing by the tiller blade,
Picking off the lice. PSSSSSSST.

You Rusty Canaller
You Son of a Bitch
Why do you follow
That dirty old ditch?

[This was a] ditty that one boatman would sing to another as he would overtake and round a slower boat on the canal. It was all in good fun, and the slower boatman accepted it in the good spirit for which it was intended.

—Simon Johnston, age 89
(From *Tales the Boatmen Told*)

When I worked on the scow, I wasn't 21. I remember John Mutchler was kind of a tough boss and when I was done, he said to me, "Next year, you'll work next year?" (I was 2l years old that fall.) I said to Mutchler, "I don't know. I won't work for you. I'll pick bones and buy rags before I'll work for you. Two or three times I caught you sneaking over the bank watching us and what we was doing when we was cutting brush. We was working hard, and two or three times you'd sneak around like that. I don't like a boss like that. Because when I work - I work!"

My father held me till I was 21 and took my wages right up until I was 21. In them days you wasn't of age and you didn't get no money till you was 2l. I think that was the best thing that ever happened because today the young kids get an allowance when they are in the cradle . . . I gave everything I made. If I went out and made a quarter, I handed it over. But when I went out to a festival or something, they'd give me something to spend. When I was 2l, I could do as I pleased. Then I quit and a fellow gave me a recommendation down to Phillipsburg on the Railroad, the ones that went out to repair on the wrecks. We had to be called out at night and I thought I could go from home. The fellow was right here on the Central Railroad out here on South Main Street. He said, "Your recommendation is good and I'll hire you. I'll tell you where to go to get board." I was going up the hill and I says to the other fellow, "I don't want no board. I'll live with Pop and Mom. I'll get a job." I came back and told him and I'll bet that man jumped two foot right in the air and swore and says, "Your recommendation ain't worth nothing." And I says, "Okay." And I went home. I stayed with my father and mother right up till I was 32 years old—then I got married. I got a job in the Ordinance. When I got home there was this job, but I only worked two days and was laid off the rest of the week, so I went to the Edison and got a job there (at $1.20 a day).

You take the hatchet and I'll take the saw,
And we'll saw off the legs of me mother-in-law.

Another ditty that although it sounds kind of gruesome, it brought smiles to the faces of children for which it was intended.

—Charles Snyder, age 89
(From *Tales the Boatmen Told*)

I liked to be on the boat and I liked to go from one end of the canal to the other; from Phillipsburg to Jersey City Basin. . . . [I was] about 12 . . . I used to wash the dishes and cook. You had a little stove in the cabin and it had a big furnace near the hinges of the boat. . . .

I drived sometimes for exercise. Then when I got tired I got on the mule's back. . . . Katie and Jenny. Jenny was a kicker. I couldn't touch her. But Katie, I could climb up on her back and ride for a while. . . .

There was quite a few black people, but I can't remember their names. . . .

Yessir! [My father] was a good man. . . . He would do favors for anybody and help anybody. He was that type of person—very good. White or colored, he would do you a

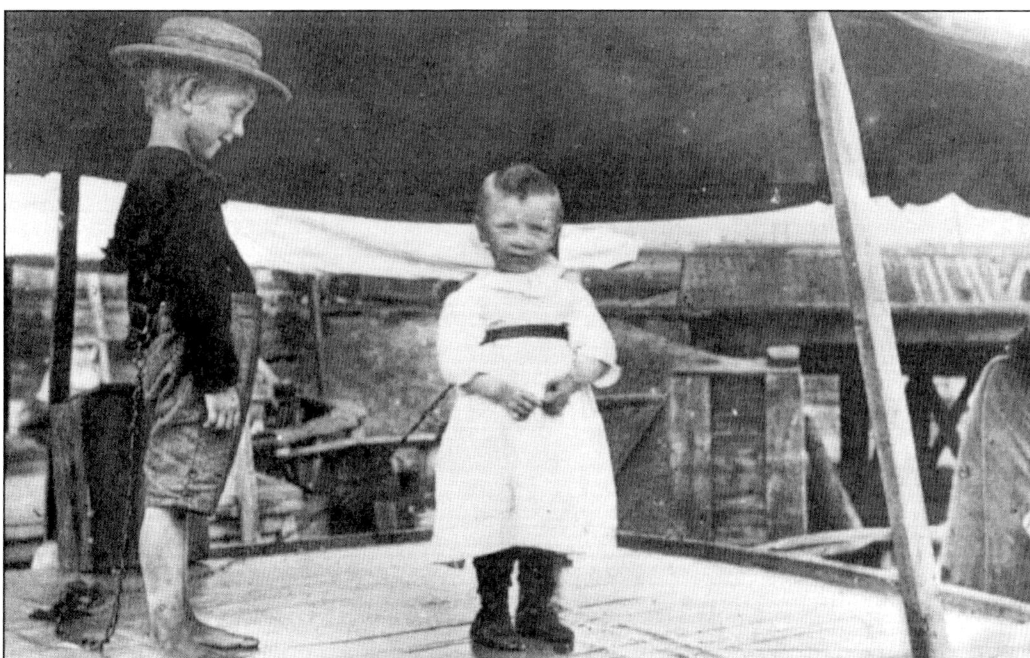

Wives tied their children to the towing post or deck to prevent them from falling into the canal.

favor. Yessir. He was a nice man and he worked in the church. . . . And then after he got off the canal, he worked for the Canal Company for a while after he stopped boating. And then when they cleaned up everything and got rid of the canal, he worked in Washington for the Water Company until he died. He always followed the water. . . .

[The boys and girls in those days] were wonderful, wonderful. I had nice colored boys and nice white boys too. 'Cause I went to Taylor Street School and they were very nice to me. There was only just a few nasty people that would call you "nigger" and chase you and try to fight you. But another bunch of white folks would take up for me. Walk me from Taylor Street School down to the corner to see that I got home. I had lots of white friends in my day. Girls used to come and play jacks with me on my porch and I used to go to their house and play jacks. . . .

At closing time for the boats when you put your mules in the company stables, well, generally at those locks or planes most of them had a little store where they sold soda and candy and stuff for the boatmen. Whenever we got there around stores I was right with the gang. We was all out there. They had jew's harps, mouth organs, and bones. . . . And they would get out there by the store and play that music and all us girls would dance. . . .

Go Along Mule

A Man in Boonton pulled a gun
And took a shot at me.
But when he took the second shot,
I passed through Port Moreee.

Go along mule
Don't you roll those eyes,
You can change a fool, but a doggone mule
Is a mule until she dies.

My father, he used to go fishing a little bit. But I was against fishing! . . . I was teached not to; teached from young in Sunday school not to fish on Sunday. One day I went fishing one time and they told me I caught the devil. The devil would say, "Take me home, cook me, and eat me up." And that they told me when I was young and I was against fishing. . . . I was teached in Sunday school to remember the Sabbath Day and keep it Holy and not to fish and not to work. I didn't mess that. I kept it all the way on the canal. I kept my commandments with my church.

[On Sunday] I just fixed something to eat. We didn't have time to get much through the week. They had bacon and ham and eggs through the week—something quick. But then on Sunday, you always try to make a stew or make pudding or something, you know, different to cook . . . and salt mackerel. We used to buy them by the pail. They called them kits. A kit of mackerel and you would keep them down by the hinges.

Only once in a while this big fat lady and little skinny man . . . got in a fight and she would beat him up. They had a lot of children, a lot of babies on the boats. And they had babies fastened to the cabin with the chains so they wouldn't fall. And he would get in a fight with his wife and she would beat him up. And sometimes he would have to jump in the water! To get away from her. . . .

Oh, for goodness. O Lord, I would have been the one to drown if I fell in because I can't swim . . . Oh . . . my brothers died. They never got on the canal. Beautiful brothers I had. We had a boy that worked. We called him a boat hand. You know, to drive the mules and take care of them like that. But we didn't have no boys, just my sister. She was like a boy. We called her "Tomboy". She like to climb and drive the mules and take them around better than me because I was kind of slow about that. . . .

At Guinea Hollow Dam it was raining and Mother told us not to run. We was on the hinges. That is the stern part of the boat. And the bow was on the other side. . . .

We were coming along fine, but a rain came up and made the—what do you call the running board?—it made it slippery. She said, "Don't run" and my sister didn't listen and didn't mind and she run, she run ahead of me and plunged into the water. And scared me to death. And then I got up there and my pa jumped in and he could not manage with a coat because it was a big overcoat he had on. And he had to go to the towpath and get the overcoat off. . . . And he got up on the boat to take the coat off. He got the pike pole. I called it a pike pole. A great big long pole—it has a hook on it. . . . Now, he kept hollering, "Hanna, Hanna! Steer the boat! Hanna, steer the boat!" And she did make the lock. And he stayed back there and got her with the pike pole there from her dress.

He could have hurt her with that pole, but he managed to get her with the dress and pull her out on the towpath. Then the man, the Lock man, Mr. Burd, was it? I can't remember too good names. He came on down and helped roll her over the pail and give her whiskey and got her together so they could put her back on the boat.

. . . There was never no trouble [between the white captains and the black captains]. No, 'cause when a mule or a horse would die there on one of the boatmens, why, then the other boatmens would try to get together and get him a substitute right away and try to help him. . . . They were a good kind. . . . Anyone sick on the boats, they helped.

. . . I was happy. I didn't have no troubles like I'm having now. No, I didn't have no bills to pay and I didn't have no nasty people around here like there is now. Everything must

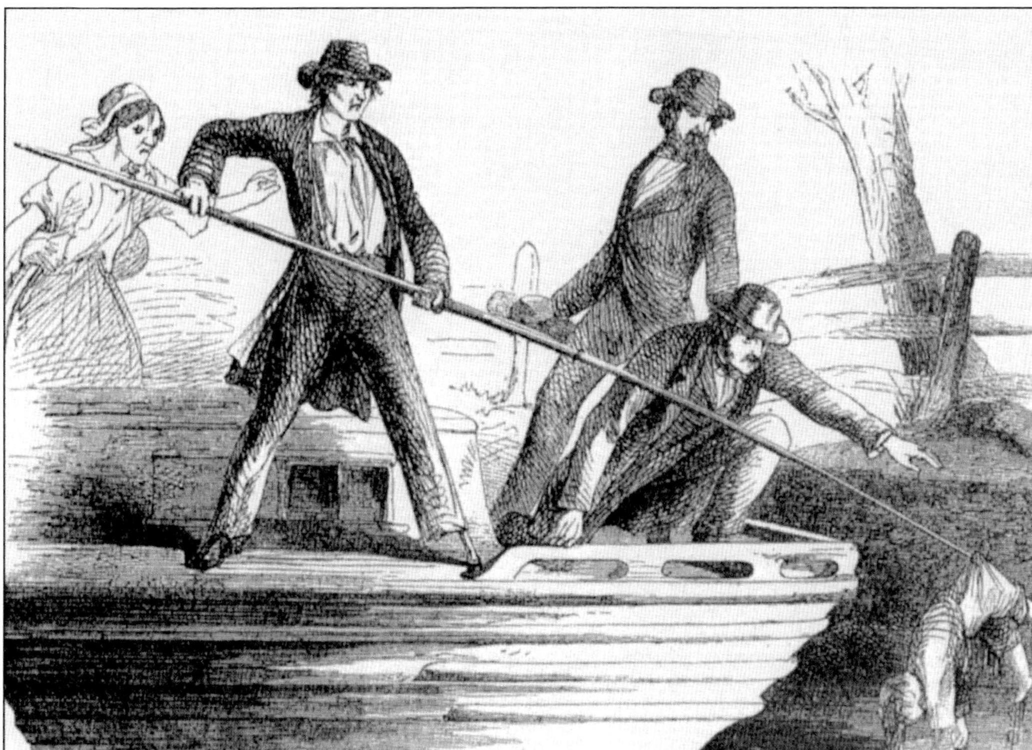

Boy overboard! The pike, or boat pole, was a versatile instrument. Many lives were saved because of its availability.

be locked up. You can't have nothing out. It is miserable for me now. . . . I am alone and they did come in and climbed my upstairs window and robbed me.

They took my clothes, money, and my best everything. Pictures and everything. . . . Years ago you didn't have to nail your windows down. People used to have screens in the windows.

. . . They were nice in my day. I had no trouble.

—Florence Van Horn, age 85
(From *Tales the Boatmen Told*)

I used to go down to the canal, and they had big places underneath where they put the mules and equipment and used to cook there. The bums would get the sterno and pour it through some bread. Then they'd drink the alcohol. Not me, no way. I never tried that. I'd just stay around and listen. I was in my early teens. That's where I learned to swim. There was a seat on a cut-off tree, which was about 50 to 65 feet down, above a deep hole, and the kids used to dive off that thing. A friend of mine got killed because he came up and hit his head. I learned quite a few little sayings and songs from the bums:

As I awoke one morning
The jailer came around
With bread and some coffee
That weighed a half a pound

The coffee was like tobacco juice
The bread was hard and stale
And that's the way they treat the bums
in the Morris County Jail.

Charlie the bum, Charlie the bum,
Charlie the bum is he.
He hangs around the corner
As happy as can be.

The other day I met him
I never met him before
I asked for a job
Picking iron ore.

I asked him what the wages were,
And he said, 10 cents a ton.
Go on, go on, you son of a gun,
I'd rather be on the bum.

—Vincent Melillo

Chapter Four
Coming of Age

Boonton Was an Iron Town
The town of Boonton acquired the name Boone-Town *c.* 1761. David Ogden, father of Samuel Ogden, a prominent Newark lawyer and a member of the provincial council, had taken ownership of the ironworks when Thomas Boone, the new royal governor of the province, arrived in 1760. Peter C. Wendt Jr., in his book, *Boonton Was an Iron Town* (1976) wrote, "Those circumstances support the Ogden family tradition that the village was named in honor of the new governor, and the governor's transfer to South Carolina in the fall of 1761 makes the year the plausible one for the name to have been given." The article indicated that neither the name Boone-Town, nor any of its variants—Boontown, Boonetown, Booneton—has been found in writings before 1771, the year Samuel Ogden wrote it as Boon-Town.

—Compiled by Janine Mellini, *Boonton Daily Record*

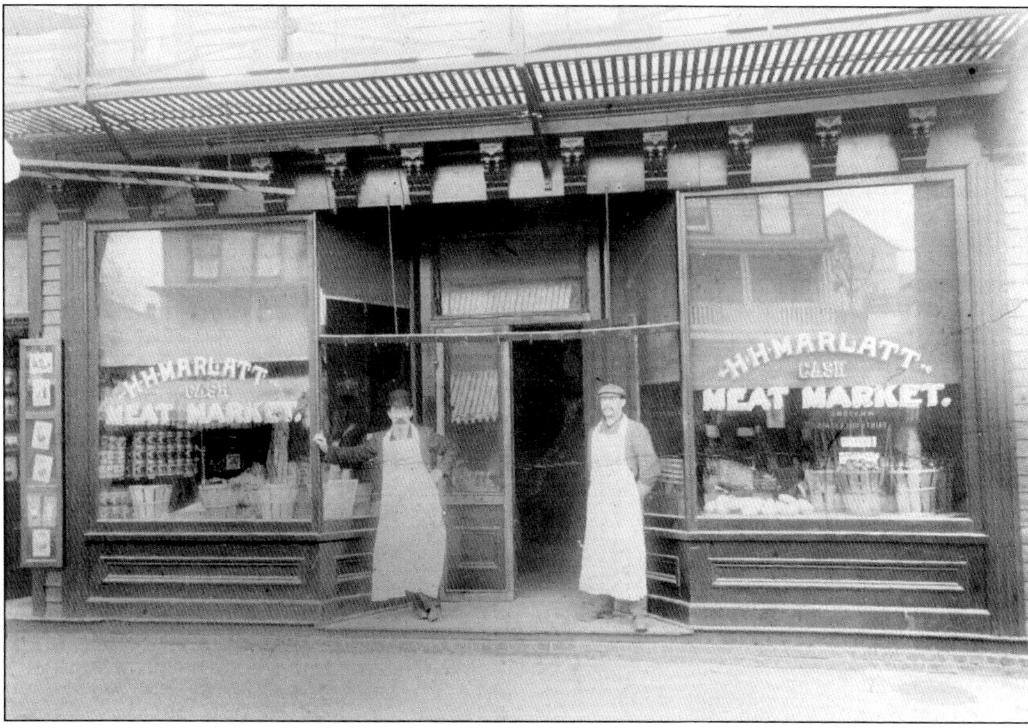

The H.H. Marlatt meat market on Main Street, 1895.

My father, Edward Henry Marlatt Jr., liked to talk about his grandfather, Henry Marlatt. [My great-grandfather] was of French Huguenot descent and moved his wife and five children to Boonton in 1885, brought them and their belongings from Hackettstown on a barge on the Morris Canal. He was attracted to the growth and prosperity that was happening in Boonton toward the end of the 19th century. Here he opened a meat business and built a home on William Street. As a child he had been apprenticed as a wheelwright and after the Civil War ended he became a teamster, because he could repair wagon wheels. When he built his house he also built a small barn to house the team of horses he used for his delivery wagon, which is still standing. My great-grandmother only lived for two years in Boonton. She died in 1887, and my great-grandad bought the family plot in Greenwood Cemetery on Washington Street, which my family still uses.

My mother, Edna Decker Marlatt, would tell me stories of how the gypsies would travel through Boonton by caravan, and would encamp on the top of Sheep Hill. Traveling around was a common practice of gypsies in the early part of the 20th century, and for centuries before that.

A Boontonian would usually spot the caravan on the road outside of Boonton and warn the townspeople. Mostly they felt the gypsies couldn't be trusted and were told to "hide their children and chickens." My mother never believed this, and the gypsies never caused trouble. They would usually spend one night on Sheep Hill and move on. Some of the Boontonians, adults and children, would sneak into the woods and watch as the gypsies danced around their bonfire.

My maternal grandmother would tell me of the hobos who would travel along the railroads and jump the cars to stop in Boonton, looking for a meal. Many of the women would leave a meal for them on the back porch of their homes. My grandmother, who lived on Myrtle Avenue, would hear a knock at the back door facing the railroad track.

She would peer out, then instruct the hobo not to come into the house, but stay on the back porch, and she would bring a meal out to him. They were always polite and grateful and would be on their way soon after. My grandmother, being of English descent, was carrying on (as were other women in town) the old English tradition of having food available for wayward travelers and indigent people who would come to your door.

—Edward Marlatt

My great-grandfather and his brother came from Ireland. Their name was Cullen, and they were farmers. When they arrived at Ellis Island, New Yorkers were trying to sell property in New York for farmland, but my [great-great-] uncle said, "No, no. We want to go inland."

So they took the Morris Canal and landed in Boonton. They were driven by mules, and as you go through the towns, they had these areas where the mule would be removed and a fresh one would be put on. They arrived at Montville and they found a property there which they bought. And my great-grandfather Dominick said to his brother, "Listen, we'll split the property for farming." And his brother agreed and said, "Well, which half do you want?" As they were going to be dairy farmers Dominick could see that the lower section would flood in the spring. But he was also smart enough to know that whatever section he wanted, his brother would think he was being outsmarted, and would want the same section. So he said he wanted the lower section, and sure enough his brother wanted the same. So Dominick conceded it to his brother. And sure enough, it flooded every year.

Much later my great-grandfather had this dairy farm and he had a horse-drawn milk wagon. He was diabetic and lost his sight. Even so he had this milk route and he would come up into town and make his rounds.

The horse knew exactly what the milk route was and where to stop. When he stopped, my great-grandfather, blind as he was, would get out and deliver the milk. His last stop was Our Lady of Mount Carmel church.

Now when my great-grandfather wanted to go to church on Sunday, the horse didn't know it was Sunday. He made all the stops he did on the milk route. And my great-grandfather would get out and get back in just as he did during the week, and the horse would continue on until they reached the church. That was the only way my great-grandfather could get to church.

My grandmother remembered the blizzard of [18]88 when they had these humungous drifts. I remember her saying that on the farm she'd go in the front door, up the stairs, and then slide out the second-floor window all the way down.

She also told me that when she was pregnant she went down to see her mother at her house on 160 Lake Avenue. She was sitting on the porch behind my grandmother, who was in her rocking chair. She rocked over my grandmother's foot which resulted in a black-and-blue toe. And when my mother was born she had a black-and-blue toe. It's very true that things like this happen because when my mother was carrying me she had her hair done, a permanent wave. At that time they would put these electric curlers on, and they would put material or cotton behind your neck to protect your neck from the hot rollers. Once it burned her neck. When I was born I had the same burn on the back of my neck that she had when she was carrying me. So it just goes to show that things happen to women when they are carrying their babies, that have an effect on the children when they are being carried.

—Corita Forrest

Six years have passed since the family history up to my birth on September 23, 1913 was recorded. Now halfway to my 81st birthday, I must try to complete the story covering my lifetime to date, if it is ever to be done at all.

The William Street years, as I remember them, probably start around my 4th birthday when my sister, Margaret, who was born February 28, 1915, was already two. There follows some of these very early recollections.

Going for rides in the Jefferey, a seven-passenger touring car, which Father purchased in 1915. Long trips, 80 miles to Walkill and Newburgh to see our relatives, the Deyos and Carvers, as well as Grandmother Sillick.

Some of these trips would be over dirt roads with frequent flats and blowouts common. Father would repair the flats on the spot. When returning home at night a bed would be made for Margaret and me on the floor in front of the back seats. At times we would be caught in a sudden rainstorm. There would then be a wild scramble on Father's part to snap on the side curtains and occasionally put on the chains, for the tires in those days lacked any real thread.

Of course, windshield wipers were unknown as well as heaters and air conditioners. In cold weather, the passengers would be wrapped in blankets, and Mother would often have the stones from our fireless cooker at her feet for extra warmth.

Going to Fairwold to see "Ba" Messiter, then bedridden. Sometimes we would go via the Fairwold horse and carriage and on rare occasions, in the winter, by sleigh. One great item of interest to me at Fairwold was the wind-up phonograph and records of all the then current World War I songs.

Exploring the woods and brook at the end of William Street with Curt Grothman and Carl Dorman. From the age of four or five there were no restrictions on my wanderings although I may have been told not to go downtown. We had great fun collecting frogs and crawfish.

At the end of William Street lived Gil Telfer, considered a very good stonemason when sober. I can still see him staggering home on a Saturday afternoon, sometimes not making it and sleeping off his drunk on the terrace in front of our house. When Prohibition came along he and his friends turned to canned heat, which eventually killed him.

Sleigh riding. There was a gentle slope in the driveway between our garage and the street, and negotiating that on my sled may actually have been my first memory.

There was a depression between the driveway and the house, and on one occasion it filled with water and froze making a nice little skating pond for the older kids. Coming down from the garage on my sled I hit Mary Conners (now Mrs. Elliot Richmond), knocking her legs out from under her. She landed on top of me and at the time it was difficult to convince me that she hadn't chosen her landing place on purpose.

—From *The William Street Days*, a diary by Jack Sillick

The Flu Epidemic of 1918

I have no recollection of this, but 1918 was the year of the terrible influenza epidemic. I am unaware that any of our friends or acquaintances died but the family was much concerned. As a precaution, Father upon returning from New York each night would wash up and change all his clothes in the garage before entering the house.

—From *The William Street Days*, a diary by Jack Sillick

People just died after a few days. Young people . . . mothers and fathers of young families. Next door, Andy died on Sunday and his wife died the next, leaving two small children.

Across the street, a lovely girl, 24 years old, she died, her brother died, and up the street, Peggy's mother, Mrs. Zayac died. And a man on the next block, John Corvi, he died. It was really dreadful. And it was the only time I ever remember the churches were closed. People didn't have gatherings of any kind. We were not allowed to go out of the house, or off the property.

And when this girl across the street died, her mother had the flu, and she couldn't get up to do anything for Ethel. When she died, of course everybody was afraid.

You weren't supposed to go to any funerals. It was so contagious. But my father did. My mother would cook and he would take the food to these homes where no one was on their feet to do anything. They were all sick or had passed away. He just couldn't stand not to go, you know.

He was a very charitable person. Mom was very charitable, too, and they just couldn't stand by and see people needing something that they could do. It was a terrible thing.

The funerals were held in the home. Not because of the contagion. But only a person who had absolutely nobody was in a funeral parlor. My mother and father were buried at home. I never was in a funeral parlor when I was growing up. You went to the home. They had crepe on the door, always with black ribbons. And there was no refrigeration, no air-conditioning. And it was usually three nights. Everybody would sit up all night, with the open casket.

—Irene Dunn

My sister caught it, and they didn't have anything to combat it. Those germs were infiltrating the entire world. Our own servicemen in France. People in New York were wearing surgical masks, all the military men.

—Stephen Bolcar

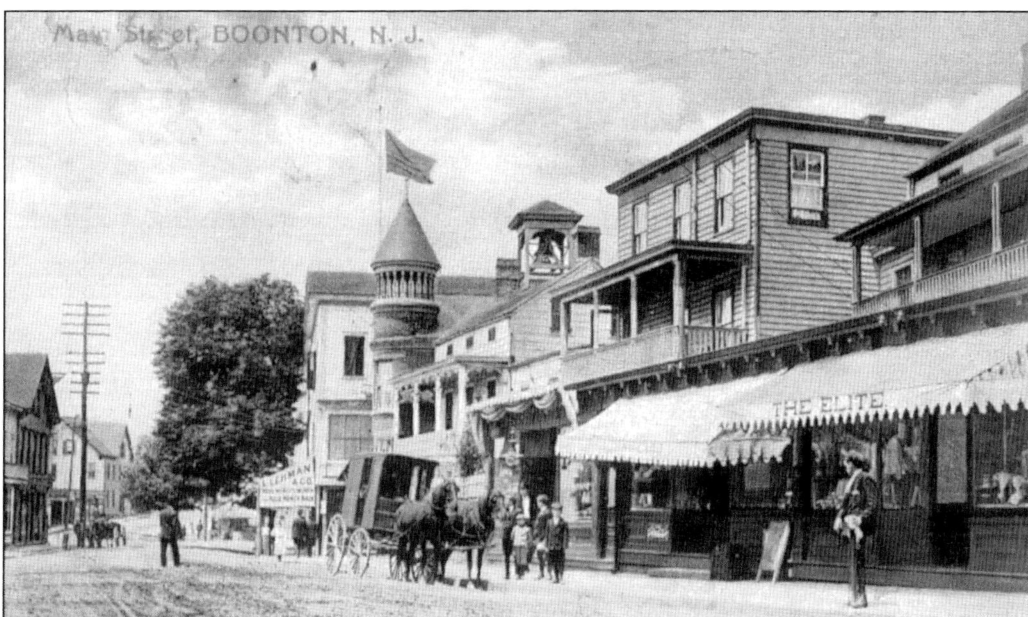

Old Main Street, Boonton.

The flu epidemic had a big effect on me when I was growing up. My mother died of the flu. I never even knew her. I never even seen a picture of her. The only thing I know about my mother [I learned] from Helen Dunn and her sisters in Boonton. Helen remembered when I was born and when my mother died. I don't even have a birth certificate, just my baptism record.

My parents had five children. My stepmother, Mrs. Melillo, had three children, and then there were the children she and my father had after my mother died. I could see in a way why they put me in a home because they couldn't actually care for all the children they had. It was hard for all the families then, and them being foreigners. They were born in Italy and couldn't speak English. My father was a mason—that speaks for itself. In other words, if they needed someone to lay bricks or plaster or stones, he was the man to do it. You didn't have to know too much of the language.

I grew up in the orphanages. I did have a family, but I didn't realize it when I was young. The only family I did have was in the home with the sisters. And they did treat me real good. It was home to me because I didn't realize what the world was like on the outside. That's probably why the army felt so much like family.

I was at the home at Villa Cono with the sisters of St. John the Baptist in Gladstone, New Jersey. I made my first communion and confirmation there. One thing I remember was that one night there was a big fire at the home.

It was real cold that night, but we all went outside when the fire started. But it was so cold that two or three of the boys went back in and died in the fire.

The sisters used to take some of the boys . . . into New York sometimes for dinner. We would stand on the corner and beg for money. What I remember most was Child's Restaurant, where they had a seven-course dinner, and it was real good. It didn't cost much because you had these little bowls of soup and dessert.

I learned how to play the bones in the home. I just picked them up one day and started playing them. They would take these rib bones and take out the bone marrow and make them hollow. Then they would start clapping them together. And I picked it up. Anytime some music was playing I'd just get a pair in my hands and clap them together, like . . .

A shave and a haircut . . . two bits
Who you going to marry . . . Tom Mix

—Vincent Melillo

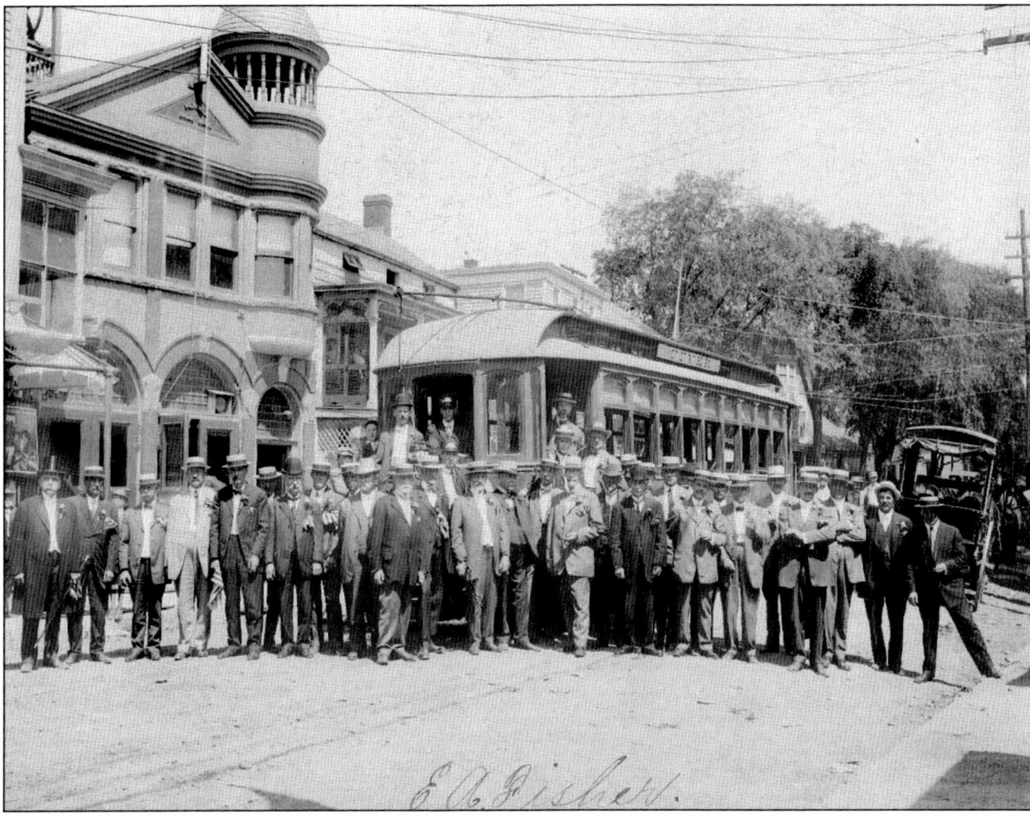

Official opening of Boonton's first trolley car, 1910.

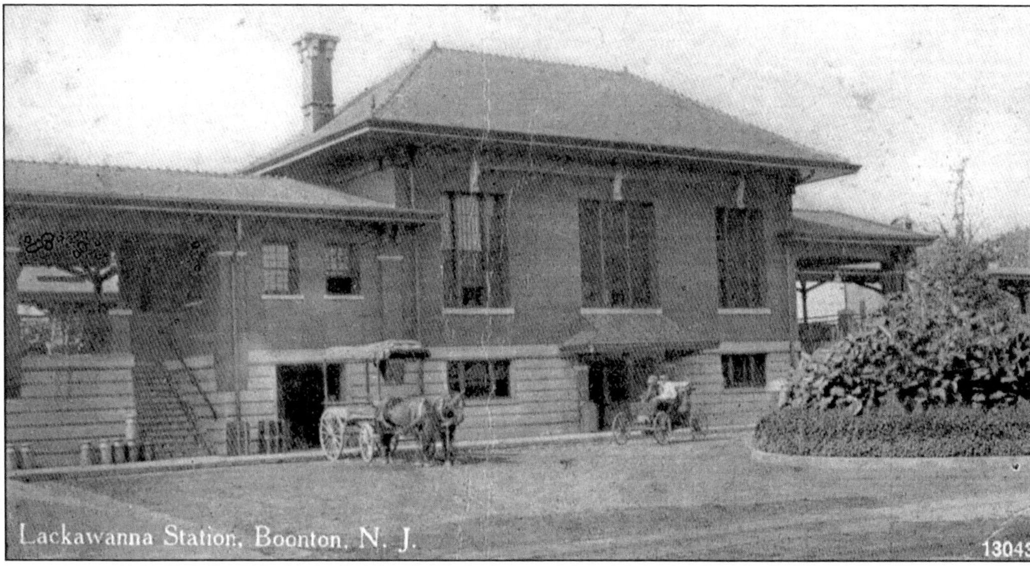

The Lackawanna station.

The reader of this account of my William Street days might be interested in what the town of Boonton was like in the second decade of the 20th century. All of the streets except for Main Street and a few others were dirt. Main itself was brick with a single trolley track running up the middle. It was tight going when vehicles were parked on either side with traffic going each way and a trolley car too. Automobiles were few in number and there were still many horse-drawn wagons. There was much home delivery, the butcher with his wagon or truck coming by a couple of times a week. He would often give us kids a hot dog which we would eat raw. Then too there were the milk, ice, and coal men. If a cellar were

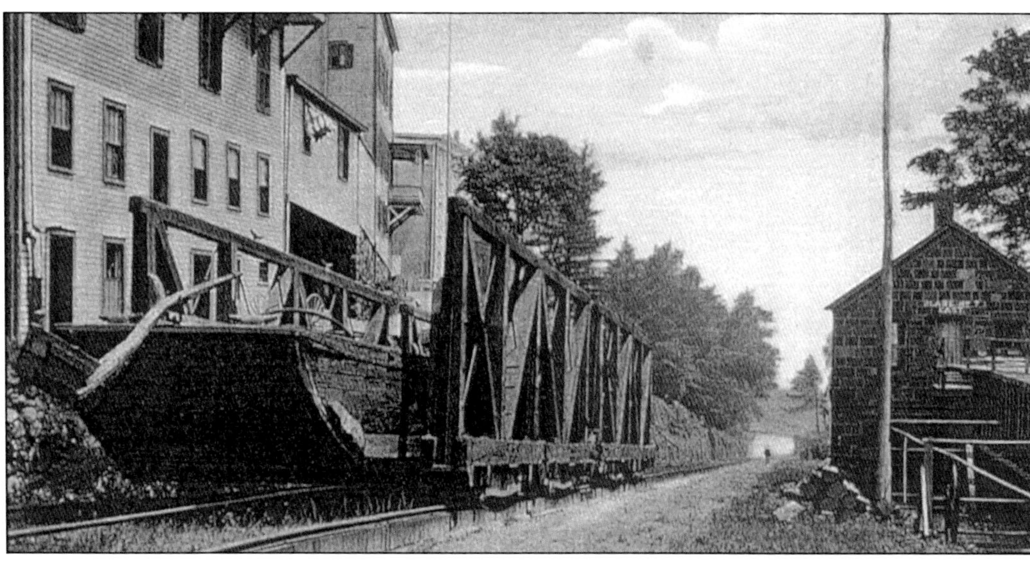

Looking down the plane.

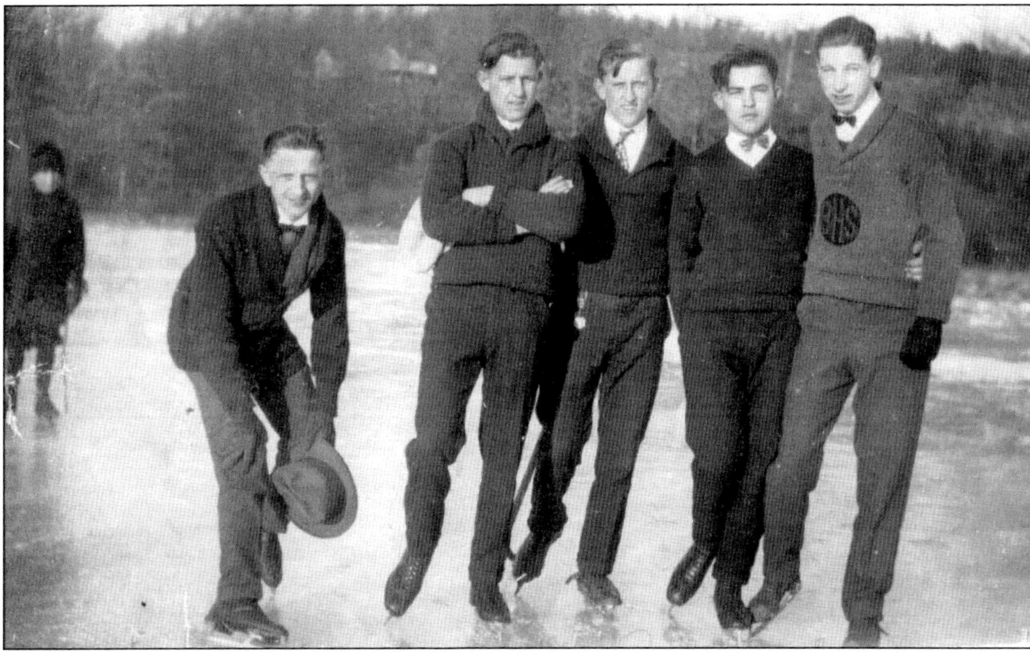

Skating on Hillery Pond.

below street level the coal man would set up chutes to slide the coal through the cellar window, otherwise he would have to lug the stuff in big shoulder bags.

At Division Street the trolley turned off Main and went to the end of the line at the railroad station. There the operator or conductor would flip the trolley pole and take over the controls at the other end of the car to start the trip the other way.

The trolley continued through Mountain Lakes using as a right of way what is now the walking and jogging path along the Boulevard. In Denville, about where the A & P is now, was a transfer station. There the Boonton line ended and you could take another trolley either to Dover or Morristown.

I believe the Dover line went beyond that town all the way to Lake Hopatcong, while at Morristown connections could be made which would eventually get you to Newark.

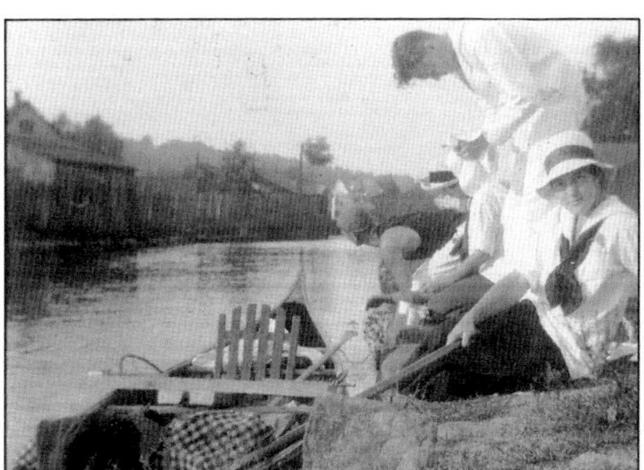

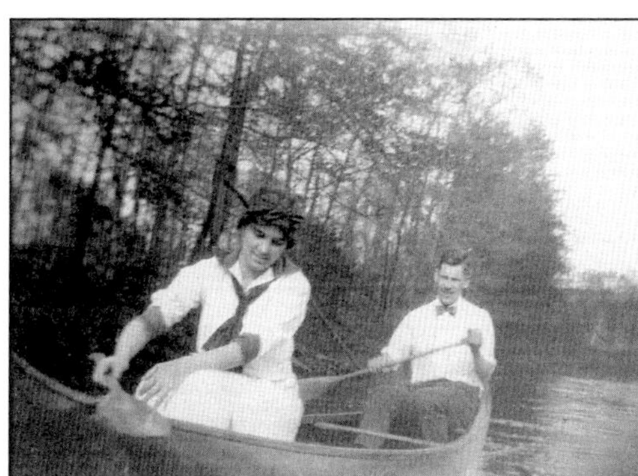

Outings on the canal, 1914.

In the [19]10's the Lackawanna Railroad was the main means of transportation. The passenger station, between Division and Myrtle, was well maintained with flower beds in the middle of the parking areas on both sides of the tracks, and well-manicured lawns on the Division Street side. In the station was an office for the baggage master. He was a busy man because in those days before UPS most everything was shipped by railway express. Perhaps there was not even the parcel post. The freight station on Morris Avenue was also a busy place. . . .

Many trains went through Boonton, both passenger and freight. A noon train, which made connections in Buffalo with another train coming from Chicago, carried an observation car.

The Morris Canal was very much in operation. It ran along Myrtle Avenue, and near where the high school is now there were locks. At the intersection of Main and Washington Streets with Lathrop Avenue, the canal widened almost to a pond, enabling two canal boats going in opposite directions to pass one another. It was good for skating and was the site of my first attempt in that activity. My first skates had clamps and straps by which they were fastened to my shoes. They were forever coming off and took much of the fun from the sport. I was probably 12 before I was given my first pair of shoe skates. I don't ever recall seeing a canal boat go up the inclined plane at the end of Plane Street but it was not unusual, the boats in Boonton and elsewhere pulled along by mules. In earlier days when the traffic was greater, people would make deals with the boatman for all day outings with picnics on board. . . .

Mary Bellamy, who came with the family from Brooklyn and did much of the housework, telling us Uncle Remus stories of her early life in North Carolina. They covered everything from ghosts to panthers (painters, as she called them). Mary also read to me from a child's story of the Bible. I credit her with my learning to read before I actually started school.

Mary had a room off the attic on the third floor. She had a great fear of thunder and lightning. During a storm at night she would come down and sit at the foot of the stairs to be near the family. One of Mary's exploits which I heard about later was saving the life of Rachel Riker. She and the other children were playing near a bonfire which was visible from the kitchen where Mary was working. Mary saw Rachel's dress catch fire. She picked up a rug, ran to the child, wrapped the rug around her, and rolled her on the ground.

Rachel was badly burned and carried scars on her body for the rest of her life. Over the years I have seen Rachel around town. She never married and died within the past year at the age of 84.

Mary's wedding was one of my very vivid William Street memories. She had a beau, a Mr. Timmons, who lived in Dover. They would meet on Sundays in Morristown where they attended church, going there by trolley. There was no black church in Boonton. Timmons would also come to call occasionally, visiting with Mary in the kitchen. . . .

When Mary announced her intentions to marry and move to Dover the folks decided to give her the wedding and reception. This must have been in 1919. Margaret was the flower girl and I was the page responsible for carrying the ring. There were probably 50 to 75 guests, all black, and the minister from Morristown. Outside on the porch, which ran in the front and on one side of the house, were many of our neighbors to view the festivities through the windows. My memory of the ceremony is dim but I recall that chicken salad was served during the reception. Father's account of the ceremony, repeated many times over the years, told of the minister obtaining the ring from me and holding it up for all to see. He then intoned "This ring is a perfect circle, 360 degrees. Now there are 365 days in the year and this means that for 360 days Mrs. Timmons can trust Mr. Timmons, but for the other 5 days she had better watch out."

After her marriage we used to stop in Dover to see Mary and on special occasions she would come down to see us. She never had any children of her own but she always seemed to be caring for the children of others. Mr. Timmons didn't stay around long and when Mary died, probably in the early [1950s], his whereabouts were unknown. Mary was one

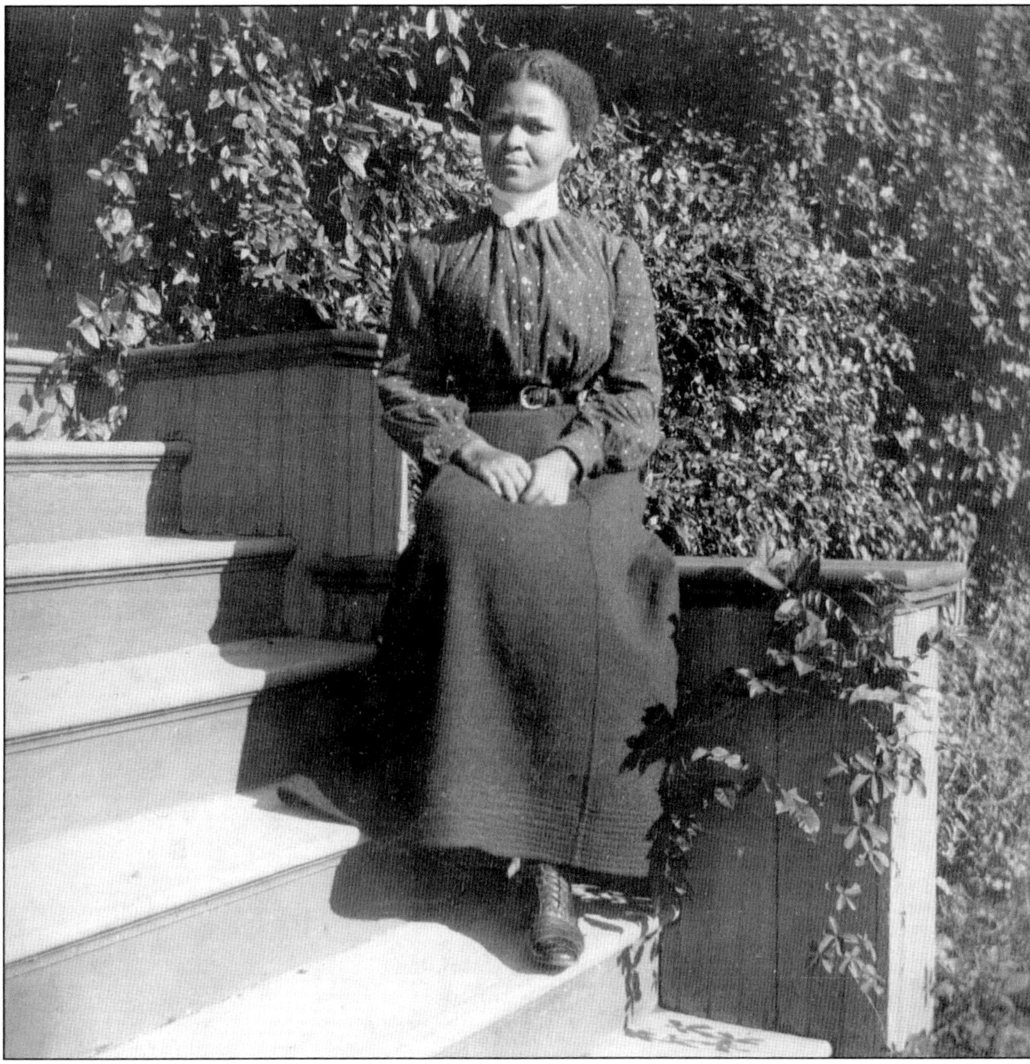

Mary Bellamy.

of the most loving and unselfish persons I have ever known. Mary always worried about my future. There was something about the moons in my fingernails which foretold that I could become a bad liar.

I was too young to appreciate what our involvement in World War I was all about. One effect on us was that Mary left us sometime in 1917 to return to North Carolina and operate her brother's farm. He had been drafted.

My folks never expected to see her again but one day early in 1919 she showed up unannounced ready to go back to work. She was welcomed with open arms.

I do have a recollection of the Black Tom explosion, an act of German sabotage, but am unsure whether I actually heard the blast or whether I heard others talking about it. Another memory was visiting some kind of military encampment, perhaps the National Guard in the Pinebrook section of Montville.

Without doubt my most vivid memory related to the war was the false armistice, which occurred several days prior to the actual armistice on November 11, 1918. The church bells rang all day. That din was augmented by the banging of the fire gongs throughout the town. There was no central fire whistle but at various strategic locations these fire gongs were set up on heavy wooden frameworks. A sledge hammer was chained to the framework and a considerable bang was achieved when the gong was struck.

—From *The William Street Days*, a diary by Jack Sillick

The Prall house is just across the street from where I live. It was built in the early part of the century and was the first house lit for electricity. It was pretty primitive at the time. They wired the house, but they didn't wire individual rooms. People would gather outside the house just to see Mr. Prall come home in the evening, turn on the switch, and watch the whole house light up.

—Jim Monaghan

Julia and Irene Dunn:
There was a piano in every house. Because when your friends came, there was music. We'd stand around the piano and sing. And our parents too. Pop liked to sing. There was no radio or television then. We were our own entertainment. And then our grandmother died in 1916. And the mourning began. There was no more piano playing. And so my sister's lessons stopped. They really went into mourning. I thought it was so foolish. My mother used to say afterwards she was so sorry they did that. But that was the custom. You didn't

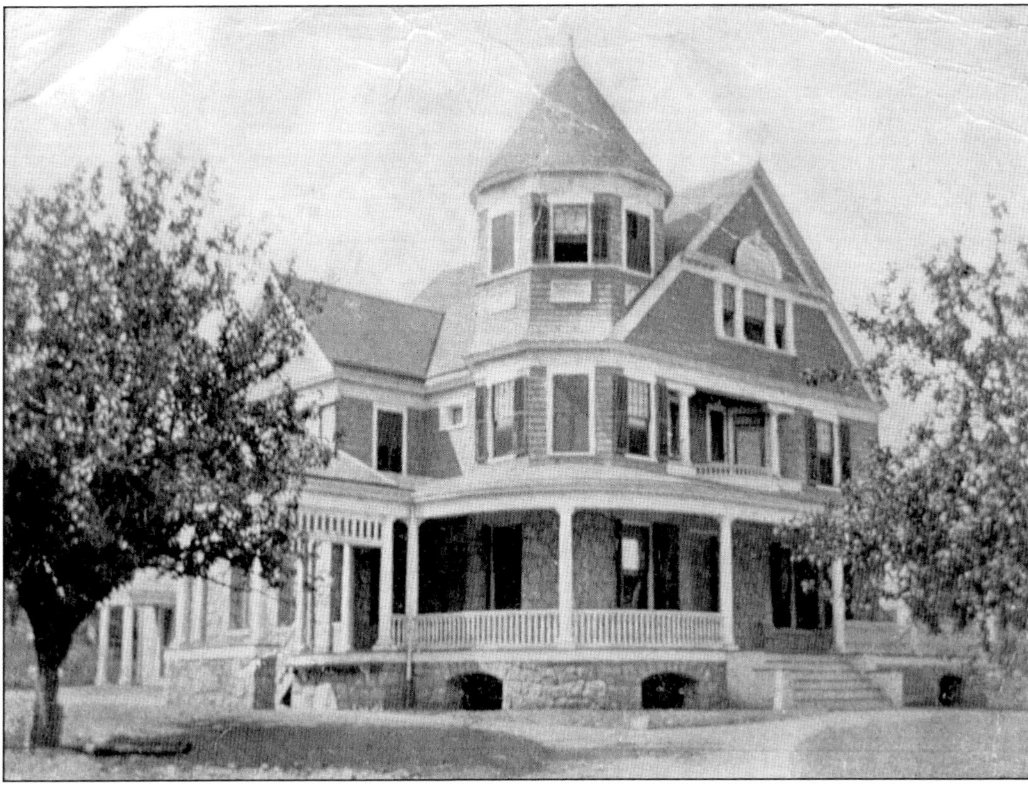

The Prall House.

play the piano or anything, because the mourning period was a long time. I remember that for the first year after my mother's mother died she and her sister wore black when they went out. And the next year they wore black and white. The women used to wear heavy veils . . . mourning veils.

The big event of our childhood was the fire department parade and the picnic . . . and Memorial Day.

—Julia Dunn

Oh, that was a very big day.

—Irene Dunn

Big parade! And we used to have Civil War veterans—the older gentlemen. Now there's hardly anybody from World War II in it. They used to have big parades. They were very civic-minded about things like that.

They marched on Main Street. The firemen wanted to pass every firehouse [laughs] so they'd start on Cedar Street, go up Boonton Avenue past their firehouse, go down around and finally end up on Main Street to go down south Boonton, and then very often they would march back up again.

And there was the centennial. They had one night dedicated to the different mayors of Boonton. They had a fashion show of the old costumes.

—Julia

And then there was the contest for men's beards. I think they said there were 400 men. [Laughs.] It was fun.

—Irene

And some of them kept them. [Laughs.]

—Julia

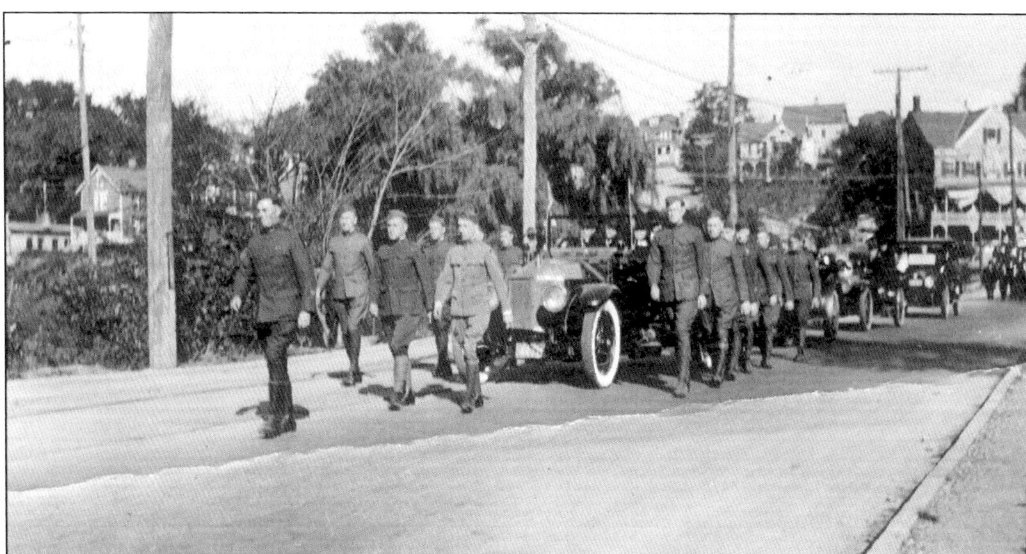

Memorial Day parade of World War I veterans.

Men's beard contest during the centennial celebrations.

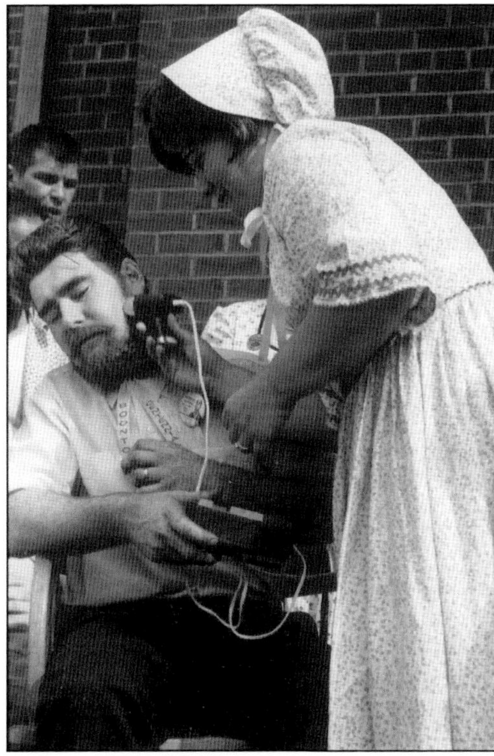

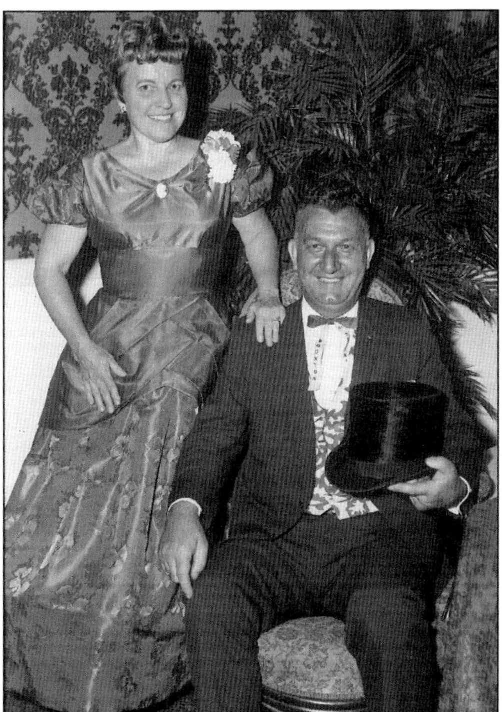

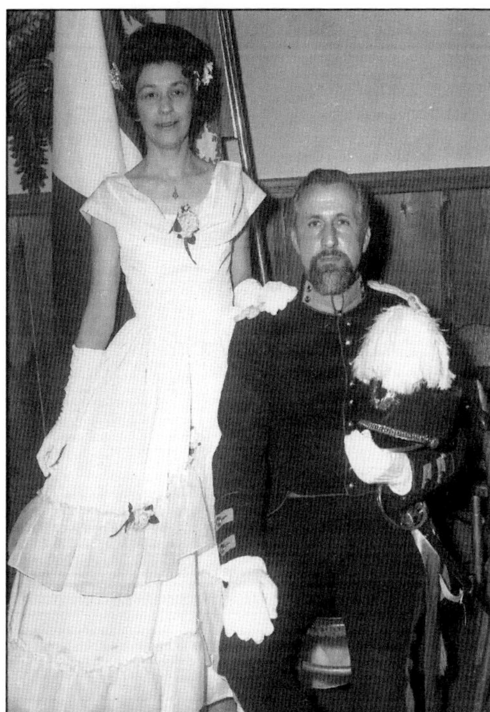

Smitty and Tony Marcello (left) and Evelyn and Arthur Eckardt (right) during the centennial celebrations.

When I went to New York City to look for a job, I had to pay an employment agency. They gave me a card and told me where to go. So I got on the subway and I rode and rode, and finally I showed the conductor my card. "Would you please tell me where this is?" And he said, "Little girl, you're in Brooklyn." Instead of paying another fare to ride back I walked 16 blocks. I carried my lunch with me. And I didn't stay in New York any longer than I had to. We wore gloves and hats on the train, and let me tell you, we had to wash those gloves each night to clean the soot off from those trains. I worked about a year in New York and then I got a job at Van Raalte.

—Arline Dempsey

I was born on a 144-acre dairy farm in 1911 that my father bought in 1846. We delivered milk in Boonton for 40 years. The Depression didn't affect us that much. Milk was our income. We delivered milk to Boonton, Mountain Lakes, Troy Hills, Parsippany. This was real milk, raw milk, before you had it pasteurized. Set the milk on your doorstep every morning for 10¢ a quart. Sundays, Christmas Day, New Year's Day, every day. We didn't get any electric lights on Parsippany Road until 1932. A coal furnace in the cellar, a coal range in the kitchen, kerosene lamps.

I got the tax bill from my father's desk in 1915. It was $56 a year. In 1936 the state bought most of the farm for Route 287. I had to sell the cows, of course. I was very fortunate. I got a job at the Morris County Park Commission. I was the ninth man hired in 1938. Mowed lawns with a lawn mower over 12 feet wide with a tractor all around it. In Morristown, around the parking lot at 25 mph.

I got complimented many times at what a good job I did. One week I mowed north and south, the next week I mowed east and west. I mowed huge areas of grass and when the terrain was right, I mowed criss-cross.

I went to a two-room schoolhouse, four grades downstairs and four grades upstairs. My father went to the same school in 1895. We walked to the school about a mile and three quarters each day . . . five-year-old kids. We went to school for readin', writin', 'rithmetic. They go now for football, baseball, and basketball. That's all they care about now.

I was born, I say, in the latter part of the horse-and-buggy days. Few people had cars. I got my driver's license in 1929, but at that time I didn't even want one because I rode a horse. I once rode 65 miles on horseback. And then I got a motorcycle. I never had an accident. I drove a motorcycle even faster than I ever drove a car. The 1934 Harley-Davidson [had] a sidecar and a reverse gear in it. I never owned a new car. I bought my first car in 1930, the 1926 Dodge Roadster. Four years old. Cost me all of $25. I had lots of cars in those days. Now you can't do it. I'd like to buy a used car right now. I got an '80 Cadillac out here that's a gas guzzler. I'd like to buy a smaller car. You go to a dealer now, "No, we don't take any old cars."

—Charles Bates

I was one of 11 children, and I worked on our farm in Montville when I was nine years old. I was supposed to go to school but I could never go to school during the month of June and the month of September, because at the end of May you started planting beans and carrots, and you had to weed that stuff for a whole month. And in September we were harvesting potatoes and tomatoes because winter was coming.

I never graduated grade school. I couldn't go to school graduation anyway because I was working on the farm. . . . I didn't have time to feel bad. It was just something I had to do.

My dad was an old lumberjack. We only saw him about five months a year, from March to November. He was always out in the woods. We had a 32-acre farm and that's where

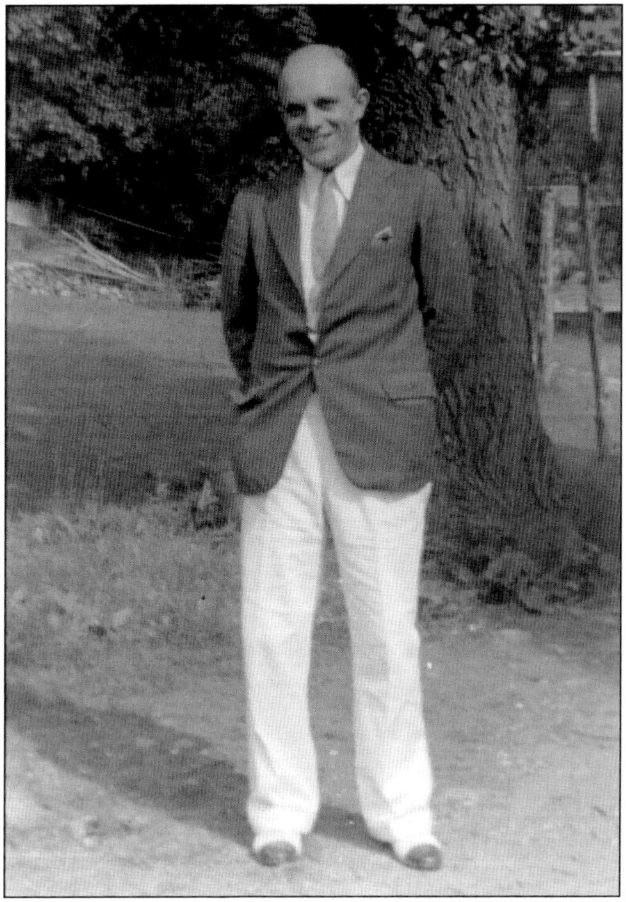

Charles Bates.

my mother and the 11 kids lived. We used to hate my father coming home. Every time he did, my mother would get pregnant. We had enough kids in the family. What we didn't have enough was food.

My kid brothers and sisters were lucky. We sold the farm and moved to Boonton in 1919. Instead of my going to school, my father bought the Treadway Trucking Company and wanted me to work for him as a driver. So when I was 14 or 15 years old I started to drive a truck. Good thing there was no policemen on the road in those days. So I used to leave Boonton at seven o'clock in the morning and get to catch the ferryboat at 11.

I was making deliveries for E.F. Drew. My dad did the trucking for them. They manufactured vegetable and cooking oil and shortening. I went every day. There was no power steering, two brakes on the rear wheels only. After a while I said to my dad, "You don't need me. For this work you can hire a jackass. . . ." So I left my dad. I got a job right away as a sewer of clothing for dolls, and then I went to work for Van Raalte as a knitter of silk stockings at $29 a week, and I worked there until 1957 when Van Raalte closed.

There was no such thing as seconds at Van Raalte. If you made a mistake it came out of your check. We were all piece workers. When we couldn't get any more silk from Japan because of the war we went on to what you call gumsilk. It was artificial made by DuPont.

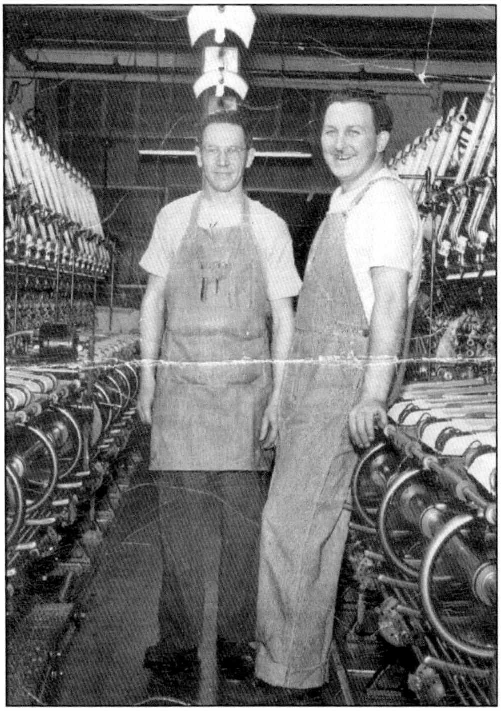

Bill Mitchko (left) and a co-worker at the "legger" machine at Van Raalte Hosiery Silk Mill, 1947.

It took a year and a half to get the machine adjusted properly so I could make six pairs of stockings. And when I got the six pair done, it took six girls—short, fat, tall, thin. These six girls had to wear these stockings every day in the week to see how long they would last. And they wore them two months. The company didn't like them to wear too long or they would be out of business.

At the same time as I was working for Van Raalte, I was also driving a truck after 11 o'clock for my brother. He was a supplier of molasses for the sneaky pete gin mills. We'd make four to six trips a day to Hoboken and load on a thousand pounds of molasses in the dump truck and put coal bags on the top so everyone thought it was coal that we were loading.

I'd be working on the hosiery, and at 11 o'clock at night the sheriff's office would have a man out in front, shouting, "Hurry up, Bill! Hurry up! So-and-so still needs 1,000 gallons of molasses. The man can't wait all night!"

I'd just come out, get up on the truck, and be back in Boonton by seven o'clock, so the next driver could load up all over again. This was the Morris County Sheriff's Department running the operation.

—Bill Mitchko

My father told me that since large numbers of immigrants had moved to Boonton from 1900 to 1920, with the building of the Jersey City Dam/Reservoir and the Boonton factories, which at one time employed over 2,000 people, the Klan movement had become quite powerful across the country and Boonton had a chapter. It was made up of prominent businessmen, families, and even clergy. He said they would have meetings at the Methodist Church and march down Main Street in full uniform, which he saw when he was a boy.

—Edward Marlatt

Following the war and in the early [19]20s, the Klu Klux Klan became very active in Boonton. Roman Catholics rather than blacks were the targets, for what reason I have never known. There were a number of cross burnings for purposes of intimidation but never any violence that I ever heard about. The Reverend Fountain, minister of the Methodist Church, which we attended, was a ringleader, and several meetings of the men in white were held in the church sanctuary. Father, out of curiosity, attended one of them and after it told them he would have nothing to do with their activities.

By the mid [19]20s the Klan was no longer visible, but anti-Catholic prejudice remained and was seen by Mother in some of the Board of Education members when she served on that body.

—From *The William Street Days*, a diary by Jack Sillick

There was a time when crosses on Kudorowski Hill would be burned by the Klu Klux Klan. As kids we had a little gang, and we knew that there was a Bible study group that used to meet at Ross's Hill. It was Kudorowski at the time. Next to it was another hill and the Bible class used to meet there in their uniforms, and we knew they met there because the parents of the boy who owned the land where the cross was being burned, knew the Klan was meeting there. We used to hide in the evenings and watch them make a fire and hold their meeting and go through whatever they were doing there.

—Stephen Bohacik

Before Hollywood took over the movie industry Boonton was the locale for the shooting of several movies. I was not aware of what the plots were but I remember men in white robes on horses riding up Main Street. Probably they were supposed to be Klansmen. At the entrance to Grace Lord Park, and what at one time [was] called Lovers' Lane, a several-story building facade had been erected. This was torched as part of the movie scenario and created a frightening sight to children.

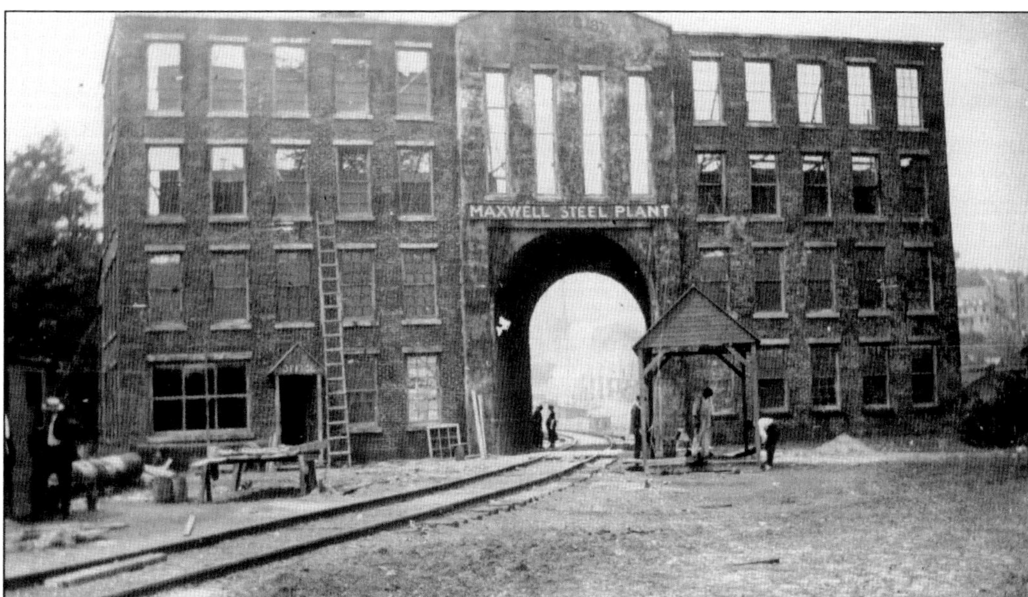

A set built for a movie filmed in Boonton, 1920.

—From *The William Street Days*, a diary by Jack Sillick
While Boonton Sleeps

A killing poison creeps down
on Boonton through the beautiful
valley of the Rockaway.
Sewerage in sewers is not
objectionable to eye or nose. Sewerage
properly disposed of may or may not look
to the eye and may or may not send forth
objectionable odors.
No one of us will ever know until
the Disposal Plant proposed by Jersey City
has been set down among us and begun its work.
But long before such an injustice
can be forced upon us greater harm will have
been done Boonton than if the completed thing
smelled to high Heaven.
But Jersey City will never harm us!
It is inconceivable that a community of
people could sit idly by and watch a great
city crush out the life of a town like ours.
Yet that is exactly what we have done and now
the last moment has arrived. We have little
time for action! But we will act!
Florrie Peer, on the property just below
the dam, has been ordered to vacate! And while
we sit calmly by and watch him go we sign our
own death warrant.
These are the things you can do now to
prevent Jersey City from forever putting a stop
to our growth and cutting down the value of our
property to the point where overnight we all lose money.
Fight the idea but fight clean.
Write to your Senator.
Arouse every one of friends and
neighbors to action.
Sign the petition to the Governor.
Read everything in the papers.
Watch the movies.
Write to the editor of our paper.
Write to the Governor of the State. . . .

In other words, get in the fight and get in clean. Don't be small, don't be petty. Talk facts and talk them hard. Boonton will win if you help.

—From the *Boonton Weekly Bulletin*, April 13, 1923

Decorated by presidents and idolized by millions, General James H. Doolittle is a true American hero. This daring pilot is best known for his World War II bombing mission of Tokyo. But what he considers to be his greatest contribution to aviation, the introduction of instrument only flying, has its roots in the heart of Morris County in the late 1920s.

Doolittle, a brilliant engineer and lieutenant in the Army Air Corps, had already won numerous trophies for flying and had set multiple speed records, yet he continued to explore new paths for aviators to travel. A true believer in taking the calculated risk, Doolittle's breakthroughs, including the first loop-the-loop flown, were not stunts. Despite the reputation put forth by the brash young aviator, his PhD in aeronautical engineering from MIT helped him calculate his new maneuvers with confidence, and full knowledge of the limitations of man and machine.

Unlike most pilots in 1928, Jimmy Doolittle believed that although it was the only method available, flying "by the seat of your pants" was not the best option for aviators. Seeing instrument flight as the key to opening new and broader paths in the world of aviation, the 31-year-old Doolittle joined a Guggenheim Fund project at Mitchell Field in Long Island investigating problems caused by flying in fog.

Developed specifically for the project, a highly sensitive barometric altimeter provided Doolittle with altitude measurements to within a few feet of the ground. To show the aircraft's exact heading, Elmer Sperry Jr. worked on the development of the Sperry Artificial Horizon and Sperry Directional Gyroscope, the descendants of which are still standard aircraft equipment today.

The other key element required was a radio beacon which would provide the pilot with a signal showing the exact place to land. That radio equipment was manufactured and installed by Radio Frequency Laboratories (RFL) in Boonton Township, New Jersey.

. . . Local residents became accustomed to Doolittle's buzzing overhead. . . . But most did not know [he] was breaking new ground.

On September 24, 1929, Doolittle went into the rear seat of his plane. . . . Seated in the front seat, safety pilot Benjamin S. Kelsey held his hands skyward to prove Doolittle was at the controls, and the plane flew blindly into aviation history. . . . Despite what Doolittle termed a sloppy landing a new door had been opened and the era of instruments only flying had begun.

—From *TelNEWS*, October 1991

Doctors and Hospitals
Julia and Irene Dunn

I graduated high school in 1932. And my mother—our family doctor had died and Dr. Griscom had come to Boonton—she went to see him, and he was looking for someone to answer the phone. She volunteered my services. [Laughs.] I wasn't doing anything. It was better than the want ads. In those days any job was okay, and I didn't want to go to New York. I didn't like that idea.

I was 17 when I started. And I've been at it ever since. [Laughs.] I was too lazy to move!

We've always had good doctors. Dr. Sommers and Dr. Noble and Dr. Arbuckle. Dr. Arbuckle was a real old-fashioned doctor. He did everything—pulled your teeth. [Laughs.]

—Julia Dunn

. . . delivered babies . . . [Laughs.]

—Irene Dunn

Irene had a medical emergency when she was . . .

—Julia

Six years old. I had diphtheria, which was a common thing in those days. It was a bad disease. Dr. Sommers told my parents I wouldn't get through that night because I couldn't catch my breath. Anyway, I don't know how they got this particular doctor. I guess he was the nearest nose-and-throat specialist. They called, and he had to come out on the train so it was nighttime before he got here. And he had to put a tube in my throat so I could breathe.

—Irene

It was quite an uncommon thing to have a doctor come from another town. It saved her life. People died from diphtheria.

—Julia

When you went to a dentist, he didn't give you nothing. He pulled out your tooth and that was it. Just as you see on TV in the westerns, that's how it was. One time I had two teeth pulled at the same time. One yank and it would be out.

The doctors used to come to the house. We had a town nurse, Mrs. Price. And everybody knows Julia Dunn. She took care of me. The doctor did everything—heart, broken bones, cold, fever, everything. No specialists at that time.

Sometimes you had to travel a long way to a hospital. Very few had cars in those days and there wasn't much public transportation. And there were some remedies your mother seemed to have. My mother used to give me kerosene and sugar for a cold. She'd rub my chest with it. And it worked. And when somebody was very sick they used to hang a sign on the door—"Quarantine."

—John Curran

Everybody went to the same dentist, Ray Spies. I went to Ray Spies when I couldn't go to the movies. My mother wouldn't give me any money because I wouldn't have my teeth cleaned. So I went down to Dr. Spies. I didn't have an appointment. I didn't have any money. I was only about 11 years old. But I wanted to go to the movies. So I went down to Ray Spies. He cleaned my teeth and I remember walking down Main Street and smiling at every pane of glass. I was so happy with my white teeth. No money. I guess he charged my mother, but all I knew was that if I didn't have my teeth cleaned, I couldn't go to the movies.

It was a simple life we led. Doctors and dentists just took care of you whether you paid or could not pay. I guess one of the reasons was that nobody left town.

There were two doctors, two dentists, no chiropractor.

I mean it was a closed community. I went into New York, and I'm telling you everyone there thought I was crazy living in Boonton. Everybody stayed here in this little, round circle, and this is where they lived, and this is where they found friends and got married.

—Corita Forrest

Years ago, every doctor's office was an emergency room because all the emergencies had to go there. When they got hurt at a factory, they all came to the office. Our office was very busy. Especially when everybody was working during World War II. Every factory was to capacity. But a lot of people had never worked before, so there were a lot of accidents. I always felt that some of the greatest people I knew were hardworking people in these factories. They worked so hard and they suffered so many injuries, poor souls, they were such good people.

In the E.F. Drew plant, where they made the edible oils, someone had to go down in those tanks and steam them out to clean them. You know, those big tank cars. That was such a miserable job. And how many were burned and hurt. I don't know how much their salaries were, but they weren't paid much.

World War II was a terribly busy time for us because we had no hospital until 1954. People who were very sick were taken to Morristown. There was a hospital in Dover,

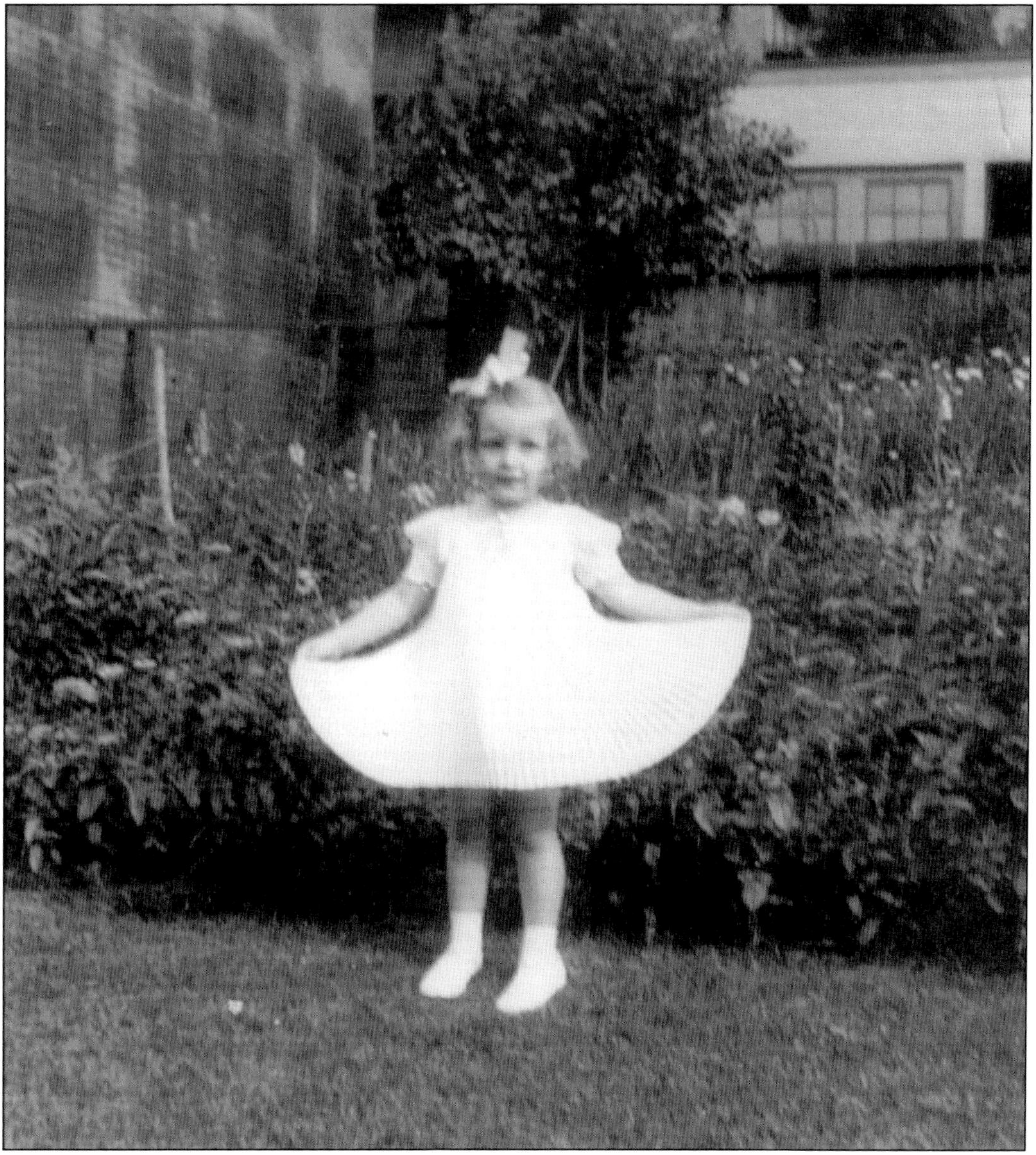

Five-year-old Corita Forrest.

but Dover was pretty crowded because of the munitions factory up there in Picatinny. It was very hard to get a patient into Dover, and Morristown was a big trip. I imagine a lot of people waited until the last moment and never got to the hospital. That's why Dr. Griscom helped to found the ambulance. He was very disturbed because he had a couple of bad accident cases and it was very hard to get the people to the hospital. He spoke to the Kiwanis about it and they decided to do something about it. So they bought a little, second-hand ambulance, and that's how they got started. Once the ambulance started, it's never been out of commission. They've run it every day since.

—Julia Dunn

Uncle Henry was one of the founders of the Kiwanis Ambulance Service in 1937. He ran the grocery store, and he was the dispatcher for the service. When a call came in for the ambulance the phone either rang in the store or in the house. He answered that phone 24 hours a day for 30 years.

When the call came in he would call whoever was on duty that night. They'd get an ambulance and take it out to the accident scene, or an emergency. And they did that up till he retired in 1972. Sometime in the [19]60s he was named "Man of the Year."

—Richard Boyd

When we came to America from Italy, we came with my mother, father, and grandmother. We lived in Roselle when I was a little girl, and my father got sick then. And he was told the doctors wanted him to give up the shoe-repair business, that it was contributing to his illness. But he didn't stop. He couldn't afford to. He found out that there was a place for a shoemaker's helper in Boonton, and that's why we came here in 1932. About a year later he opened up his own shop. He died of lung cancer. He was a very heavy smoker.

—Edith Bohacik

The doctors detected it, but there was nothing they could do about it. Because at that time there was no surgery to remove the lung. Radiation was the only thing available and it wasn't effective, even as it isn't today.

In my mother's case, this is going back to 1938, she had a disease called "pemphigus." It's a rare skin disease. I still think it's an incurable disease now, but I believe there is some treatment for it. When she was at Memorial Hospital, then where the shopping section is next to the station, her doctor asked another doctor, a skin specialist from Newark, to look at her. I always remember that one of the things he said was "Make sure you have $75 ready to pay Dr. James for coming up." That's what he charged. That was in 1938, and that was a lot of money at that time. My mother found out it was incurable. The only treatment he prescribed was that when we brought her home from the hospital, what we had to do is make the bed and put a rubber sheet down. Then cover her fully with corn starch to absorb the moisture from her body. Then lay a canopy over it. And use Christmas lights in order to heat it, to keep her body warm. And if her body got too hot, you would unscrew bulbs to cool it off.

I knew she was praying to die. I used to hear her.

Her condition was very painful. She refused to eat. Anyway my aunt, my mother's sister, had a farm. And she started to bring all kinds of dairy products, milk, cheese, eggs, and began to feed her.

It appeared to me from reading about this disease that there is a point at some time where you starve yourself and the body builds up such a strong immune system that it may have killed this disease. Because all her skin came back and she recovered. She lived for 12 more years.

—Stephen Bohacik

It must have been her faith that carried her through.

—Edith Bohacik

There have been tremendous changes in medicine. We've gone from having no transportation, no hospitals, to having good transportation and good hospitals and all kinds of care. It's been wonderful.

—Julia Dunn

Chapter Five
The Great Depression

The crash came and my father disappeared. Oh, my God, they were looking for him all over. My God, they were always showing up at the door. I knew nothing. I didn't even know who they were. I was about 13. My mother never told me why he disappeared, but I did know he was bonded. He bought everything on margin. For a long time it haunted me, and then my mother remarried after she gave up trying to find him. I never saw my father again.

When I was 18 I heard that a priest driving his car turned the corner on a red light and ran into my father as he was crossing the street. He died in the hospital about a week later.

My father was no dope. He was a projectionist in the movies. And then, my mother said, he went to work for a broker on Wall Street. He was no dope and he was making money. You said it. [Laughs.] My sister and I, who was four years older than I was, went into the city every weekend to be with Daddy. On Saturday when the Stock Exchange was only open in the morning he would take us to stand up in the balcony at the Stock Exchange, then take us out to eat where he could get a drink. [Laughs.] My father's mother was a concert pianist. We had everything, and then we had nothing.

I went to high school, 1930 to 1934. We were the "depression class." We had nothing, nothing! Really! All of us! And we only had the one bus home. To get to school in Boonton from Towaco, which was five miles away, where I was living, there was one bus to get us to school and one bus to bring us home. And if you missed that bus going home, you were out of luck. Even today I don't know how the hell I got back from school, if I missed the bus. I keep thinking of it all the time. But I remember how I got home one time. A teacher said to me, "Doris, we want you to stay after school today. We want you to do this." And I said, "Who's going to take me home?" So they went out and got, and you can't do that today, Mr. Butterworth and another teacher, two young men, they would be going around where I lived and they would drop me off. I'd sit between the two of them. I look at it today and I say, "Oh, my God. You'd never do that today. I wouldn't trust anybody today."

I was lucky. I got a job when I got out. Hardly anybody from the graduating class got jobs. I couldn't go over to County College. There wasn't any money for me. We were all very close, but nobody had any money.

I'm over there at the museum in Morristown, and they have a shop. And those kids come in with $20, and they've gotta spend every dime of it. And I'm gonna tell you, I keep thinking, "holy mackerel," if I ever had $20! I [would have had to baby-sit] from 6:30 at night till one, two o'clock in the morning. And I got a buck.

As I grew up, things began to get a little better. Before I met my husband I was going with this boy who went to Dartmouth and then to Cornell. But I got bored with him. He wanted me to go to college and I could not afford to do that. And he said, "My mother will send you." She had a lot of money. But I said, "No, thank you. I'm not going to hear that all my life." [Laughs.] So he got mad at me. I didn't care anyway.

And then at deer-hunting season we were sitting across the room when all the men were going out hunting and there was this fella', he kept looking at me, and finally he asked me if he could take me out. And I was a little bored so I said, "Oh, sure." Later he told me that when we were in high school he watched me all the time, and finally he got up the nerve to ask me out. [Laughs.] And then Slim kept taking me out and one day we went to a justice of the peace and got married.

He was the policeman on the beat. I was a cheerleader. Slim had no training in police work. You didn't need it then. Before that he was in the ice business, with Dixon Ice, delivering ice. But he was an avid reader. When he was working on the night shift, he would come home, take off his uniform, go down to Rutgers and take all kinds of police courses. Later he became the police chief of Boonton for 35 years.

—Doris McCoy

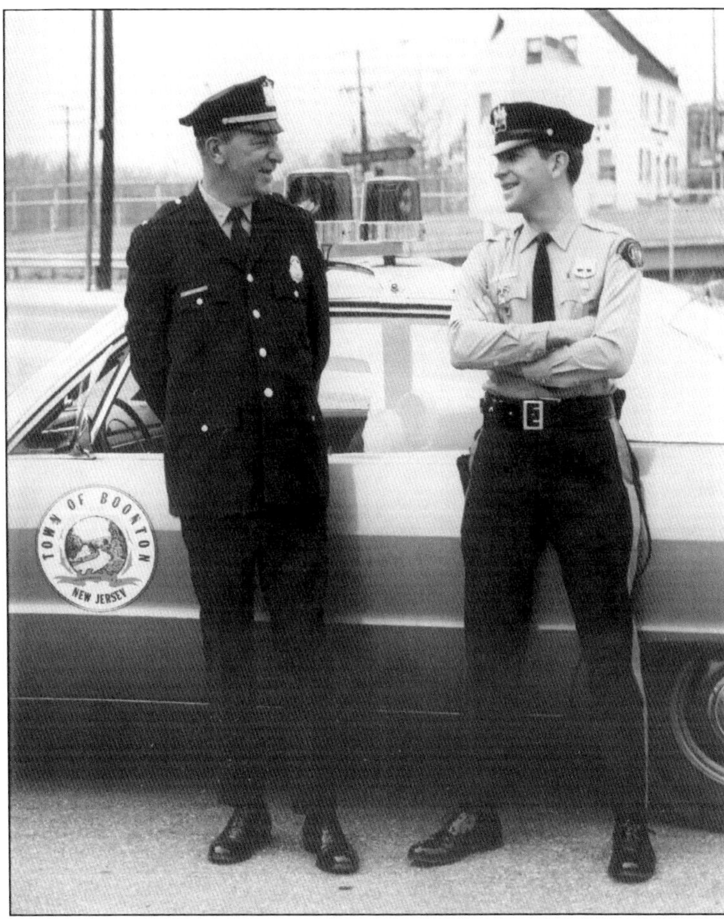

Chief "Slim" McCoy and son Charles Frederick, 1970.

I was born in 1927. The crash was [in 19]29. The Depression was through the [19]30s until the war came and pulled us out of it. It hit my mom and dad, but I didn't know about it. We were poor but I was not aware that was anything special. One day I found a letter that my mom had written to a company. She had bought an appliance on time payments and she was late with a payment. Something like $3. She ended the letter with "It's hell to be poor." I didn't know we were poor until I saw that letter. Obviously, she never mailed that letter.

—Lloyd Charlton

When our neighbor, Mrs. Baldwin, died, her house went on sale. It had been built in 1920. We bought the house. Big deal! We put $100 down and the mortgage was $3,500. That was the end of the Depression.

We just took it like it is and we didn't have any money to finish it.

—Doris McCoy

Going to the grocery store in those days, compared to now, is what slays me. You used to buy any kind of meat in the store, except high-price steaks, which you could get for a quarter a pound. Hot dogs was 25¢ a pound. In those days there was only two kinds of bread—today's and yesterday's. So if you bought yesterday's bread, it was half price. In 1936 or [19]37, New Jersey put a sales tax on everything, but it didn't last too long. I don't think it lasted a year. They took it off damn quick. Well, when they did that, if you bought two loaves of bread you were taxed. People were in an uproar over that.

My mother used to send me and a friend of mine to buy bread. She said, "Now you kids go in separately and each buy a loaf of bread. Then there's no tax.

—Larry Dixon

We were married in 1930. That was not really the best year to get married. You probably don't remember the Depression as well as I do, but it was very bad then. We lived in Brooklyn for seven years and that was really very nice, because I was from a small town. I'm a farm girl myself. My husband was not a farm person, but he liked the country. But we both felt we'd like to find something more countrified.

Our first apartment in Brooklyn was one room at $55 a month. And we lived there until our second child was born. Our second apartment had two bedrooms, but the bedrooms were too small for two children. So every Sunday, religiously, we went through the real estate section of the *New York Times*, and one Sunday it said, "For rent: 200-year-old house," and, I think, it gave the rent, which was $55 a month. So Monday I called up the real estate people and they told me how to get to the train to Boonton, which I'd never heard of. They also showed me pictures of a lot of Mountain Lake houses for about the same price. Well, that wasn't what I wanted. I wanted an old house. And the minute I saw this house, it was my house. I fell in love with it. On Wednesday I signed the lease. That was the summer of 1938.

We hadn't seen much of New Jersey till we moved here, except what you see from the Pennsylvania Railroad, which is horrible—factories, smokestacks, broken window panes, that sort of thing. It was very interesting for us to find that there were really rural sections.

A little over a year after we came here, the landlord, who was as eccentric a person as you can possibly imagine, rang the doorbell at 11 o'clock at night. We were both in bed.

We got up, came downstairs, and he said, "Do you want to buy this house?" And we said, "Well, we sure do, but we don't have any money. He said, "Well, see if anybody in your family can lend you the money."

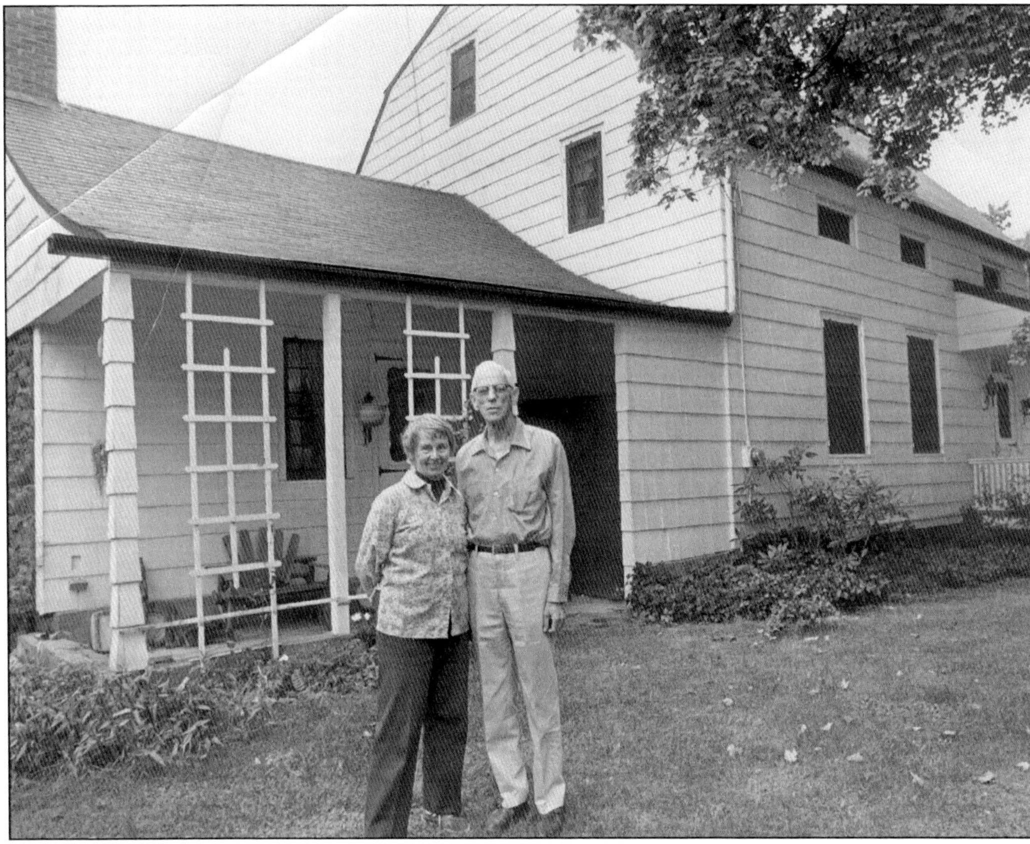

Merk and Alex Fowler in front of their Miller-Kingsland home.

He was offering it for $8,000. We could have it for half that price and the rest would be a second mortgage at four percent interest. We borrowed the money from my grandmother and father.

We've done a lot of work on the house. We're very careful not to change it too much. We always have a sense of the past. We've always felt we were custodians of it. Houses this old, many of them have been lost. The highway takes them, somebody buys them and tears them down. They burn up.

The original family that owned this house was the Kingsman family. The people in those days did not require privacy and they didn't require much furniture. Incidentally, they owned three slaves.

My father had a horse and buggy. My grandmother had her own horse and buggy, and she used to take my mother into town quite a bit. We had mules for the farm. My father was a coal dealer.

When I was about 12, in 1918, we got our first car. And my father sold our mare. And were my sister and I furious at him because Lady, our mare, was just like somebody in the family. And I said to my father, "How would you like to have somebody swap you for $1,000 and a long-haired mule?

—Mae Erskine "Merk" Fowler

The months spent digging through old, dusty deeds to uncover the history of 17th-century Morris County homes and details about the folks who lived there made Alex Fowler feel somewhat like a detective.

"It was my own house that inspired me to do this project," said Fowler, who moved from Brooklyn Heights with his wife, Merk to their landmark Miller-Kingsland House in Boonton 46 years ago. "There were two things I wanted to know—when it was built and who built it." When Fowler retired from AT&T as an electrical engineer, he had the time to find the answers. His search led him to Johannes Miller, an immigrant from Pallantine, who bought the property in 1728; Jacob and Ann Miller, who built the front part of the house, and Isaac Kingsland, who expanded it. In 1967, Fowler wrote in letters the history of the home and its personalities to each of his three children who grew up in it. Those letters, which served as an inspiration for the book, make up its final chapter.

The book, "Splinters From the Past: Discovering History in Old Houses" the result of 30 years' research, includes sketches of 61 historic homes in eastern Morris County as well as family profiles. It is illustrated by 53 prints from area libraries and drawings done by Bob Johnson of Mountain Lakes and Larry Korinda of Boonton.

His wife is responsible for editing, proofreading, and "general expediting" of the book, which includes a step-by-step method of how to do local research.

—From the *Daily Record,* March 11, 1984

Before I went to go to school I'd get up early, before the sun gets up, to pick strawberries. Sometimes I'd take off from school and stay a little longer. The teachers understood we needed the money. I got paid about a nickel a basket. I went to the little red school on Harrison Street. Later they converted it from a school to a still. Today, it's a mosque. Then I worked with the milkman. He'd drive the truck and I'd deliver the milk. I got paid about 50¢ an hour.

My father couldn't get much work and my mother was sick. A lot of the merchants would come around from the bakery and the grocery and sell things door to door. If my shoes wore down, my mother would send me to the five-and-ten store and have me get new soles.

I don't know why, but I always liked to go to the Chinese laundry and watch them wash and iron all the white shirts. Everybody wore white shirts in those days. The Chinaman had a flat table and a little iron on top of a cast-iron stove.

During this time there was this chicken man who came around with a truck. The chickens were in cages. My mother would grab one. My job would be to take it in the yard, put its head on the block, and chop its head off. Then throw it in a tub of hot water and get the feathers off.

—John Curran

Did you ever hear of a 5¢ raise? These were the raises of the day. I was out of school in the [19]30s, and there were just no jobs. I remember one of the teachers at the school where I worked who said, "You know, Dunn, if we could ever get up to $3,000, that would be great, wouldn't it?"

—Irene Dunn

I had completed the freshman year at Boonton High School and I was given a devastating blow. I was raised by my grandpeople, and I had many, many difficult roads to overcome. My father had his own family with his second marriage.

My grandfather, who raised me, said to me, "I'm going to have to ask you something. I'm going to ask you to drop out of school. I need the money." Money wasn't like you people make today. If you got $5 or $6 a week after that tremendous crash in [19]29 and the [19]30s you were lucky. Some of the fellows I knew who worked in New York City in banks on Wall Street were working for that, if they could get a job. . . .

I was 15 years old. I would caddy for 65¢. If you got a 10¢ tip that was great. I would give this money to my grandpeople. There was this general store in Boonton where customers were on the book. My first pair of shoes was $2.95. And Mr. Zucker, who was a wonderful man, would take a quarter a week to pay off the book, or whatever you could afford. I went from job to job. You'd work for six months and then you had to look for another job. And then it started to pick up because Hitler was starting to make his move in 1939, and consequently Boonton Molding was hiring. And then it was only 45¢ an hour, $18 a week.

—Stephen Bolcar

It was the Depression when I was about 12 and left the orphanage to go back to my family, my father and stepmother. Everything was strange to me, and it was pretty hard at the time to fit in with the family I did have. I had a stepbrother, Tony, that was put in a home too and a sister, Lucy, who was deaf and dumb. She was in a home, too. They both died there. When I first came back, they wanted to know who I was, Tony or Vincent, and I didn't know who they were talking about. I can't explain the feeling you have moving into a situation like that. You try to do the best you can, and when they tell you to do this or that, you would do it without question. I would get up and build a fire. We just had a kitchen stove at the time. My father cut a square on the floor upstairs and put a grate there so that the heat would rise into the bedrooms on 104 Oak Street. And then he built an oven in the garage to make bread and pizza. I would light the fire and get it warm so they could bake bread. My stepmother, Mrs. Melillo, would prepare the dough, cover it, and leave it by the stove. When she put it in the pan, I'd carry it down and put it in the oven. Whatever dough she had left after the bread was made, she would make pizzas with tomato, cheese, olive oil, and a little oregano. Sometimes I'd carry them down to the saloon on Main Street where we would get paid for them. My stepmother did all the canning for the family. We'd wash all the bottles, and Mrs. Melillo would be out there cooking the tomatoes, putting them through the strainer. We made wine, beer, and liquor. We had one of those bottle cap machines, and I'd go down to the five-and-ten and buy a bunch of those caps. After the bottles were full, I would cap them and put them in the cellar.

My father would mend the shoes for the family. We had those iron things—lasts, I think you call them. We'd go down to the five-and-ten and get the leather and he'd put the shoes together.

I picked up Italian songs from my father. You'd hear them on the radio. There were all these tenors singing and advertising Italian food. Mrs. Melillo used to love to get underneath the radio to listen to them.

I went to the seventh grade at Our Lady of Mount Carmel. It was real nice. The teacher used to put the girls on one side and the boys on the other, and we had spelling contests. You'd learn from one group or another when they were reciting things, like "Daffodils" and Robert Louis Stevenson. By the time it was your turn you might hear it a dozen times. It might stick in your head and you'd be able to repeat it when the teacher called on you. One thing I remember is:

A wise old owl
Sat on an oak.
The more he heard,
The less he spoke.

The less he spoke
The more he heard.
Take a tip
From a wise old bird.

There were games we played when we were kids. We used to manipulate strings in our hands and make things like London Bridge, a cap, a cup and saucer, or a parachute. Sometimes we worked together. I'd put the strings in my hand and the other kid would take them from me and make something of it. And we would go back and forth.

The boys played Knock on a Rock. It was played with a little piece of stick, cut down to a point on each end. And we'd play Hide and Seek, Ring Alevio, and Kick the Can. And stickball with a broom handle and a tennis ball.

That was the only year I went to school in Boonton. No one told me to quit, but times were rough. I became a laborer working for my father.

The circus was in town one night, and my friend Sebo and I got into a boxing match at the fair to make money. I won, and he was taller than me. We got 10 percent of the gate. They made $7, and we made 70¢. At the golf course we caddied for 50¢ for nine holes. At that time that was pretty good money. Sometimes you would carry two bags when it was especially busy at the Rockaway Country Club.

Another job I did for my father was at O'Dowd's Dairy. My father would go inside the silos and waterproof them so the fluid wouldn't seep out. The buildings were about 300 yards long and there were a lot of cows there. They would take the urine and manure from the cows and throw it on the strawberry fields. And I remember later the people picking strawberries.

My brother, Gus, started the taxi service in Boonton and I would go down there sometimes and wash cars.

Once I sang with Les Brown and his Band of Renown. They had an amateur night. I don't think I was too good. Later on I worked at the Boonton Molding Company.

—Vincent Melillo

You know, we didn't even realize there was a Depression. My mother and father both went to work. We had chores to do at home. And we didn't have all the new things, but we had everything we needed, good food, and we'd get a sleigh at Christmastime, which we needed desperately to ride all the way down Cedar Street and across into the coal yard, which my grandfather owned.

My father worked for Floyd W. Treadway. He moved furniture and other things, but he was also in charge of going to New York and bringing out the vaudeville costumes for the State Theater. And I was so thrilled because they would give him free tickets to go to the movies. So I didn't know we were in a Depression because I got to go to the movies. [Laughs.]

We were delighted by the holidays. We were thrilled to come down the stairs and see a sled or roller skates. And then Easter time was very exciting to me because that was the time that no matter how cold it was, Easter was the time when I took off my long underwear. I had those tiny socks on me, and my grandmother said, "She going to get rheumatism because you took off her winter underwear." [Laughs.] And on Mother's Day we did something that children don't know anything about today. If your mother was alive you wore a pink carnation to church, if your mother was dead, you wore a white carnation, and my mother had taken in a boy that lived two houses from us, Bill Sofel. His mother had died when we were in the fifth grade, and he came to live with us for a while. And my mother made sure that while my brother and I had pink carnations, he had a white carnation. And I do that to this day.

And then there was Thanksgiving. Well, before Thanksgiving, that was when the hunting season would start and my mother would get up at five o'clock in the morning and she would make sausages and pancakes, and everyone would come to our house. And my father would shoot the gun off and they would go hunting. My brother and I waited all day. We ran home from school to see the rabbits, so that he would show us the feet and we would pull on them, and they would jump up and down. You know, things like that were very big in those days because in those days most men were hunters.

Every Sunday we visited our grandmother. She had a little farm on Chestnut Street. There was an outhouse. We used toilet paper on Sunday, but during the week we didn't. We got the Sears catalogue. [Laughs.]

And then my great-grandfather owned the coal yard. We would stop at the coal yard, and my aunt would let all my friends in to get warm in the winter. Naturally, we all walked to school. There were no buses in those days. Sometimes we wanted to play hooky. I can remember one day in particular. It poured. And I walked through every puddle, and at that time I had my long underwear on with my stockings over the top. And I walked through every puddle, thinking that the teacher would send me home. Well, she didn't. She had me take my stockings off, hang them on the radiator, and go sit down with bare legs till they dry.

The movies were a big part of our lives. That's all we had because we had no cars. And my mother made me sit by an exit door in case of a fire. And in school we had a harmonica band. We had a great time in school.

When I was in high school I remember going to the junior prom. The buddy of [my date] was taking us there because he had a car. I almost collapsed when he arrived because I had to climb with my long evening gown into the rumble seat. That's how we got there. [Laughs.] Coming home, we walked home and stopped at Ratti's for a sundae. Can you imagine young people today doing this, just stopping for some ice cream. We walked all the way from the prom dance to my house in my prom dress.

So these are the memories I have of my childhood. And this was during the Depression. We didn't have all the new things, but we had everything that we needed.

—Arline Dempsey

Everything we had to fix in those days you had to do yourself. We always had to mend it ourselves, the women did. Now if you get a hole in your sock, you throw it away. But then you didn't have the money to buy new socks.

—Stephen Bohacik

You had to do with very little. But it was a beautiful life, I think. We were all so poor, we didn't realize how poor we were. We were so rich in love of family.

—Edith Bohacik

At that time, in 1930, the children also had to hustle to make a buck. In my case I started delivering papers when I was 11 years old. And I had two routes, a morning route before school and one after school. And I was making between $6 and $7 a week, counting tips and all.

Anyway it taught you to be responsible and feel you were of some value because you were contributing. And also at that time it became necessary for the people to have a garden, and chickens, and in our case, also pigs. So the butcher would deliver two pigs and

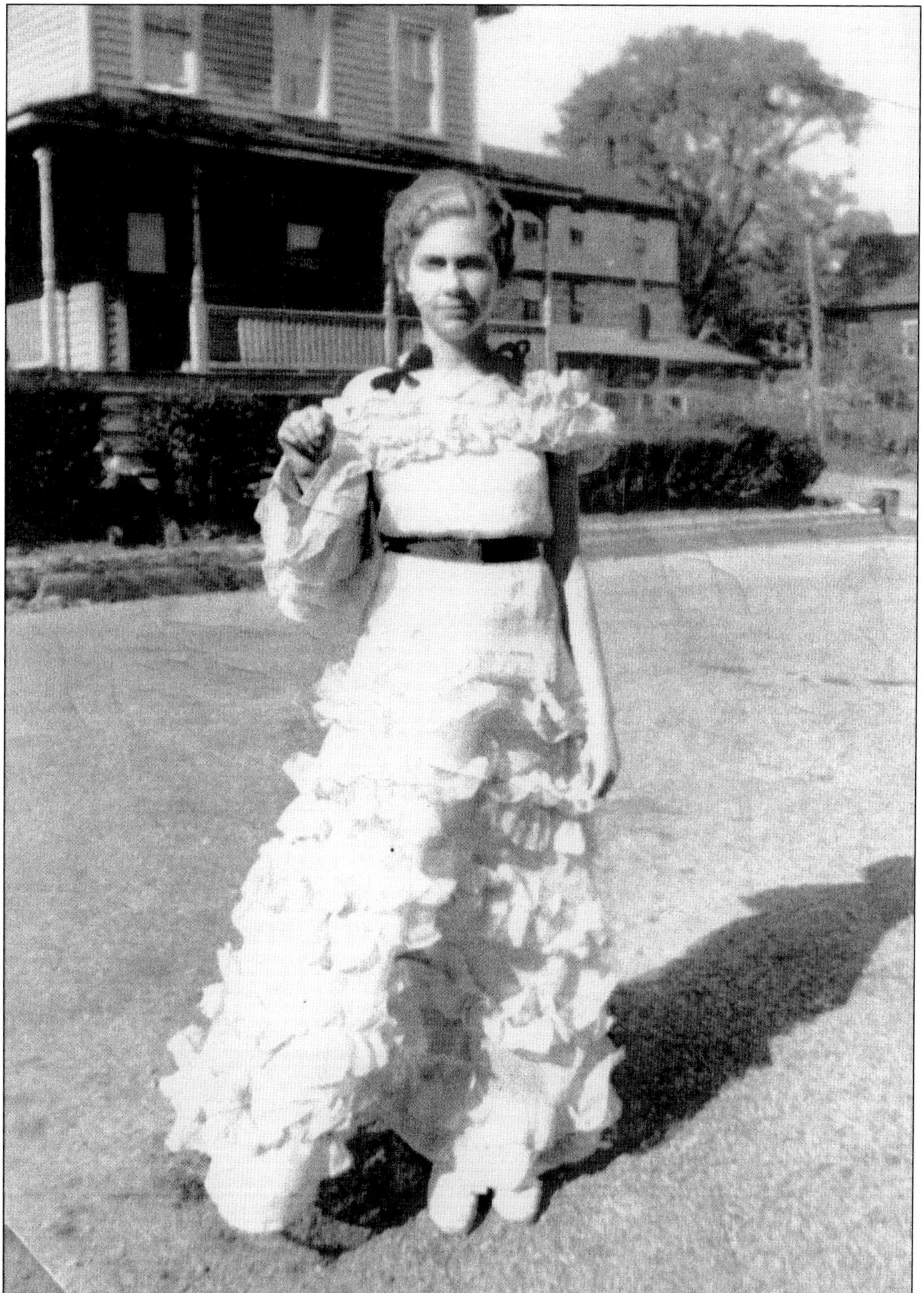

Arline Dempsey in her prom dress.

they would be stored, the hams and the bacon would be smoked in the small shed, and the white meat and the better meats would be packed with salt and garlic and covered in the cellar, to preserve it for winter use. And on the ground there would be a sandpit. We would store the carrots, the turnips, the beets, and the onions would be hung in bags from the beams, and a big barrel of cabbage would be turned into sauerkraut. So you'd have a grocery store and a butcher shop right down in the cellar

—Stephen Bohacik

And all the families would have fruit trees, peach trees, apple trees. In the fall the women would pick all the fruit and can it. I can't forget how I used to help my mother peel peaches and pears to can. And we had beautiful fruit all winter long.

—Edith Bohacik

And the canning would involve mainly tomatoes, tomatoes and peppers, but also string beans, a favorite, and fruits and preserves and jellies. And then in the summer when those jars became empty, then the root beer would be made. The same jars would be used to store the root beer, and so much gas would be created, if there was a slight crack in the bottles, you'd hear the bang, like an explosion, of these jars in the cellar.

—Stephen Bohacik

Politics

People either loved or hated Roosevelt. A doctor I worked for was such a Republican he couldn't stand the thought of a Democrat.

—Julia Dunn

The presidents I like were George Washington, Abraham Lincoln, Reagan was all right, and Teddy Roosevelt, but not FDR. He was a Communist. We called his wife "the Little Red Hen."

—Charles Bates

My mother had little respect for Roosevelt. We had a friend who loved Roosevelt. She thought he was great. So we went up to Hyde Park, and Myrtle was so happy. She went out in the middle of the garden. Roosevelt was buried there.

He gave his property to the state, I guess, or the federal government, with the understanding that everybody with the family name could live there, tax-free, for the rest of their lives, which my mother didn't particularly appreciate. Anyway, there were these two biddies out there, elderly women, who looked like they came from Boston, in their delicate, new dresses. One of them said, "Oh, isn't it awful, that poor man buried here, and not a tree to shade him." And my mother turned to them and said, "Don't worry. It's hotter where he is."

—Corita Forrest

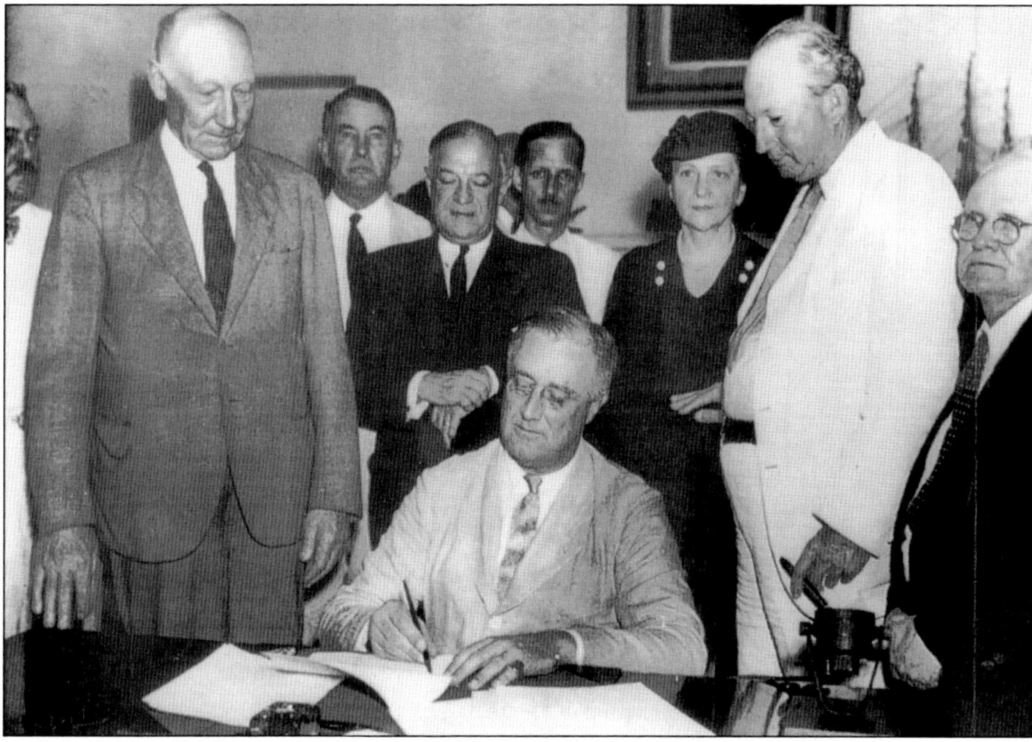

Pres. Franklin D. Roosevelt signing the Social Security Bill in 1935.

When you look at the programs Roosevelt put through—

—Julia Dunn

He was wonderful.

—Irene

He never got enough credit for all he did. Discount what he did for the war, which was tremendous—but socially what he did to help people who had nothing. Social Security. And he put people to work who were desperate. He founded the CCC camps, he got them building roads, and he got people organized. Even in a little town like this he had people working, and sewing groups to give them a few dollars. They would meet, and a lady we knew was in charge of the sewing groups, and they could make money like that. He kept musicians and orchestras going. They would go down and play at schools and other places. Just to be able to pay them something. You've probably seen pictures of those poor souls in Washington who went on the march there. They had nothing.

They were very cruel to Eleanor. Everybody was. Because she was a woman, but what a wonderful woman. She was so good. People talked to her, you know. And she listened to them and got their story back to the President. She went everywhere. It would have been a lot easier, having a big family as she did, to stay home and just be the First Lady and take it easy, but she didn't. But they were very rough on her. Nothing stopped her. She didn't care. There's no one in our office now who was alive at that time, and they think you're making up stories about how people lived, and how they worked, and the debt they owe to Roosevelt.

—Julia

Nobody was making big money after the Depression until Eisenhower came in. In 1967, I was getting exactly 65¢ an hour as an inspector. Mr. Scribner was a wonderful man but he had a group of men who were in charge, and I could see I wasn't getting anywhere in this company. Then I was hit by asthma bad. I lost about eight jobs because of asthma. My last job was as a bank courier for a state bank. I was making 80¢ an hour.

Finally, a fellow told me, "Hey Steve, they need a fellow at RFL in Boonton Township. So I got a job in there and they put me in the stock room. Mr. Seabury, the young boy who was the personnel manager, said, "Mr. Bolcar, what would you take for 40 hours?" I didn't want to ask for a high figure. I figured I was only making 65¢ in my last job. I said, "Would I be asking too much if I asked for $90?" "No," he said, "but I tell you what I'm going to do. I'm going to give you $10 more, but don't tell your friends in the plant." That was in [19]67. I was 50 years old.

I retired from RFL in 1984. And when I went to see Mr. Seabury to tell him I had to have a gall bladder operation in [19]69, I asked him, "Will I have a job when I come back?" He said, "Mr. Bolcar," he always called his workers Mister or Miss, "You'll have a job as long as you want. The only way you'll lose your job here is if you punch somebody, or if you steal our commodity and sell it to another organization." And in closing, he said, "Do you need any financial assistance?"

If I had to live my life over again I would do exactly the same thing except I would further my education. When I was having this terrific battle with asthma, my daughter was going to go back to Boston University after her vacation back here, and she told her mother she wasn't going to go back because "You need help, financial help. Pop's not working again."

At the supper table I said, "Judy, you'll go back for your junior year, and you'll finish your senior year." So if I had to drop out of school to go to work, all my three kids graduated college. I'm grateful for that.

I look at it this way. The good Lord gives us many good days in our lives and he also gives us some bad days. It equals out, you have your ups and downs, but I think the good Lord has given me more ups than downs. Many nights my wife had to stay up to two, three o'clock in the morning. I couldn't lay flat. She'd open the window trying to get fresh oxygen so I could breathe.

I don't know when I'm going. I have seven grandchildren. I'd like to see a couple of great-grandchildren come into this world, but if it's not to be, I've lived a good life. I did everything I wanted to do.

—Stephen Bolcar

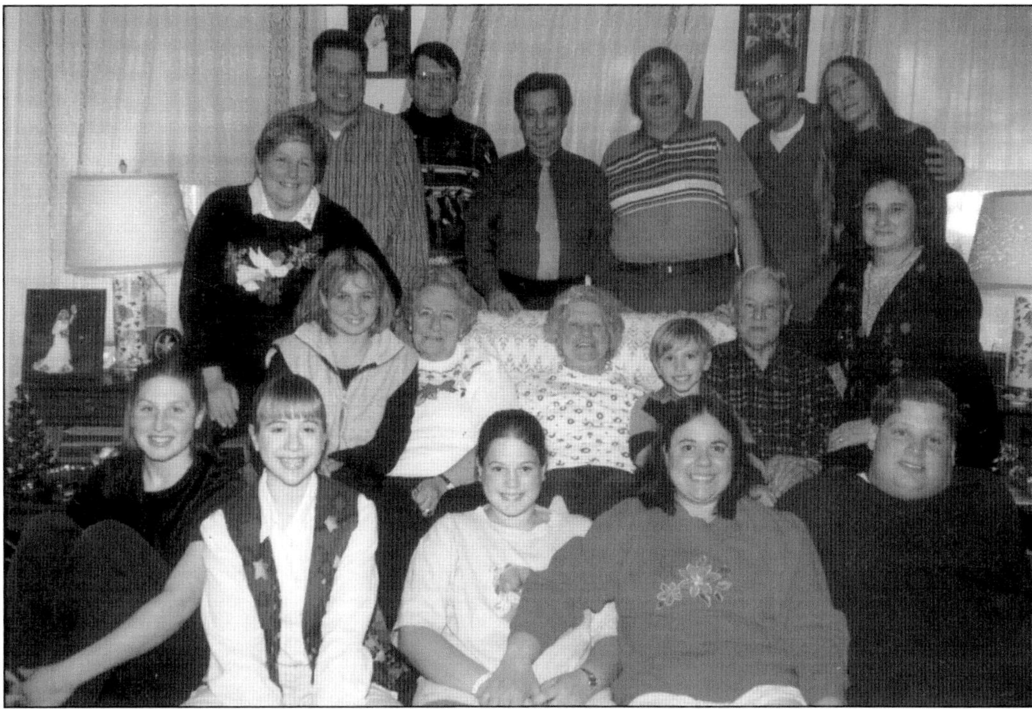

The Bolcar family. Seated at the right, in the second row, are Emily Bolcar, nephew Travis, and Stephen Bolcar.

Chapter Six
Boonton Faces the Future

Lew Abrams, manager of the State Theater, is in possession of a set of false teeth found in the theatre after Monday's matinee performance, and will be pleased to return them to the owner, if they will call for them.

—The *Boonton Weekly Bulletin,* October 12, 1937

I started at the State Theater right after high school. This part-time chance came up and I took this job. It was about four hours a day. I was 18 years old. I was the cashier, sold tickets. And I did it from 1944 to 1979. I saw most of the movies. After I sold my tickets I went inside and watched the movies. They were good movies, not what they have today.

Then they started to run X movies, and we weren't doing much business. They had a lot of out-of-towners coming to these movies. [Laughs.] The local people, I think, didn't want to be seen. We had a lot of churches in town, and I didn't like to be working there.

Business started going down. We had bad parking in Boonton. And Parsippany had a big theater. At the time of the war, we had a line around the library to Church Street and around the corner, and I sold tickets continuously for an hour. At that time there were a thousand seats. And the theater filled up.

Friday night we had a lot of trouble with the teenagers. Sometimes the ushers had to put them out.

At the very beginning, when I started, the blacks all sat upstairs in the balcony. They automatically went up there. I didn't have to say anything. It was 20¢ then. I remember one time way back, a couple must have been from New York and they wanted orchestra seats. And I said, "Well, they all sit upstairs. I'll get the manager." Well, he let them sit in the orchestra. After that they were allowed to sit anywhere.

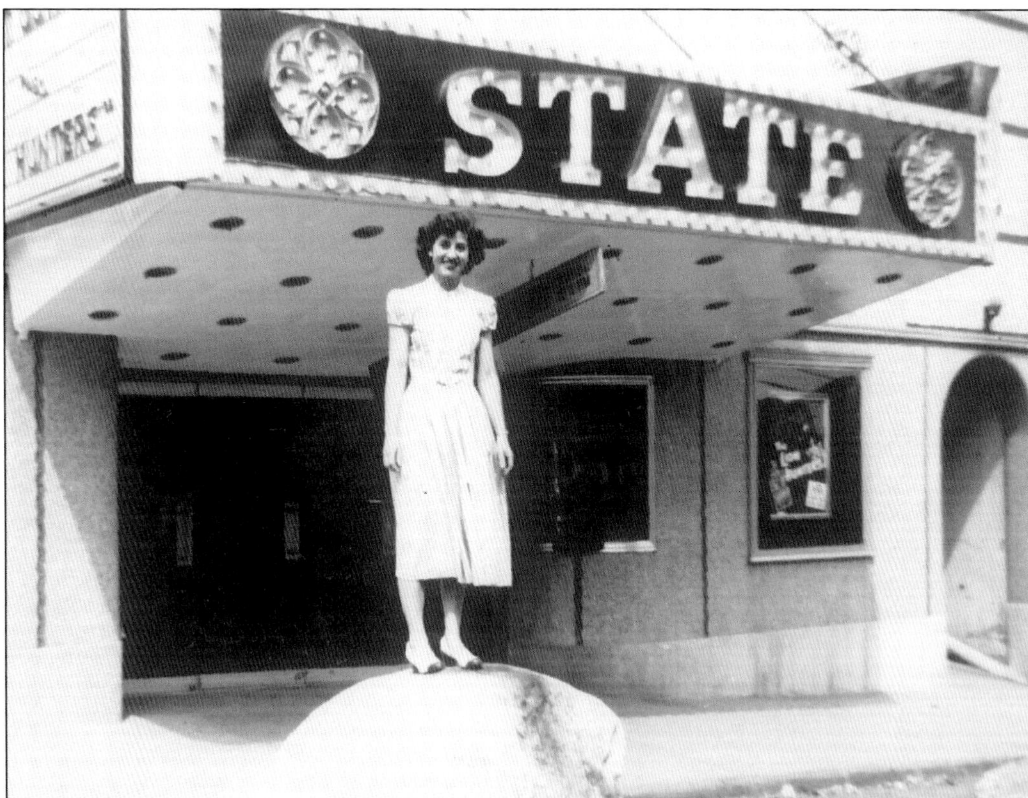

Gilda Micioni in front of the State Theater on June 24, 1951. The street was under repair.

A lot of young people went upstairs. You know, couples. [Laughs.] Just to sit in the dark, I guess. They also saved a dime.

You know when you go in, the audience is facing you. That's the only theater in the country, except for California, I hear, that is built that way. Now I always thought this was the right way. When I went to other theaters I thought they were backwards. Sometimes people came from out of town and said, "How do you get in this place?" You really go under the stage, go up and turn around to find a seat.

One time I remember the Boonton Harmony Band came back from a concert where they won trophies. They were all in uniform, about 40 or 50 of them, and they were all half-drunk. That Sunday they marched into the lobby of the theater, the whole corps of them, and started playing their instruments. And I shouted, "You're not allowed to do that!" They just didn't pay any attention.

Billy Bendnar, who was a policeman, no less, and a member of the [band] said to me afterward, "We never should have done that." And then I told it to my boss who wasn't in that day, and he thought it was funny.

In the [1920s] they had entertainers coming from New York. George Burns even said on television that he made his start in Boonton, New Jersey. And Gracie Allen. At that time they had dressing rooms and velvet drapes—not like today where the movie house is nothing but a box. We had a velvet curtain with the star of the show coming out.

And we had all kinds of special nights. There was "bank night," when people in the audience won all kinds of dishware. When there was an especially exciting movie, you would suddenly hear like an explosion in the audience. And the usher would cry out, "There goes another plate."

—Gilda Micioni

When I turned 16, I got an opportunity to work in the State Theater. I always wanted to because I always wanted to see movies [for] free, and more than once, and be paid for it. It was 25¢ an hour, but even at that it was not a bad wage for a high school kid.

The first movie I ushered for was *Edward, My Son*, and the second one was *Colorado Territory*. It's the Darress Theater now. It was the State Theater then.

George Burns came to the Lyceum at the foot of School Street, although every theater in Boonton, at one time or another, took credit for it. I heard an interview on Channel 13 and he said, "Our first booking was in the Hill Street Theater in Boonton, New Jersey." He called it the Hill Street Theater because he remembered the hills.

He came up on a bus, but unfortunately for you, unfortunately for everybody, we don't have any records or reports of it, and the reason we don't have any records of it, was because the [paper that the] theaters advertised in was a general newspaper, but there was another newspaper, the *Boonton-Times*, that was very strictly Republican and published the Republican line. But it wasn't the newspaper that everyone read. The one that everyone read was the newspaper that had everything. It had all the ads of the theaters, the stores, the stuff that was happening. We don't have a record of that because Mr. Holmes, who owned the library, dictated that [the *Boonton-Times*] was the paper the library was going to collect. The other newspaper had the whole history of the town. But they were lost because the library collected the wrong newspaper.

—Jim Monaghan

You know, in those days the cars weren't very reliable. And Mother wasn't a confident driver. Driving around Boonton with a standard transmission and going up Main Street was a real adventure. She always got stuck on the railroad bridge. You had to put the brake on, put the clutch in. You had to maneuver the brake, the clutch, and the gas pedal, the

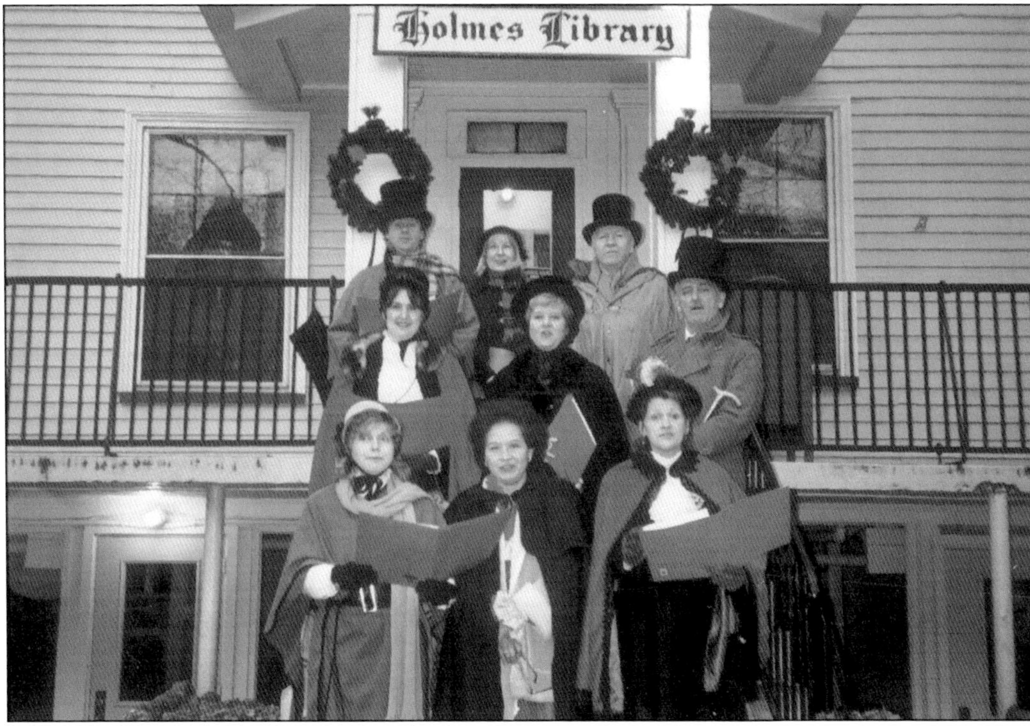

Carolers at Christmas on the steps of the Holmes Library. From left to right are the following: (front row) Mary Ellen Hart, Amor McGuinness, and Georgette Fedunie; (middle row) Bridget Burke, Micki Mollahan, and Jim Monaghan; (back row) Rob Palmer, Lucky Mascott, and Tom McGuinness.

three pedals with two feet. Get it into gear and get started. And when the light changed she'd always stall the car.

I remember just coming down the hill one time when the brakes failed on her. She managed to make it into a parking space on Main Street. But with her it was always an adventure.

There used to be a tale around here about how the steam engine blew up in town one winter. What happened was that we kids used to stand on the railroad bridge, and the passenger trains would come here and stop at the station. Then they'd start up again and stop just before the bridge. We would just stand on the bridge and chuck snowballs into the smokestacks. They had safety valves on them, we called them "pop valves," and when the steam pressure got too high, the valves would pop and let the pressure off. They'd go off like a cannon.

Anyway, about this time we were just coming out of the Depression and nobody had any money. I got $1 a month for a haircut. In the late 1940s and early 1950s, they had the State Theater uptown. I think it cost 25¢. Every Saturday morning we would go out and ring doorbells, my sister and I, and we'd ask for empty soda bottles. All soda bottles were deposit bottles in those days. You got 2¢ for the little Coke bottles and a nickel for the big bottles.

When you got enough of them you'd take them behind Henry's grocery, turn them in for cash, until we had 25¢ each. And every Saturday morning we'd go through the cushions of car seats looking for spare change until we had enough to go to the movies.

—Richard Boyd

Oh, yeah, there was segregation here. I didn't know that the theater was segregated at that time, but Don Estler lived next door to Gloria Conn. He asked her to go to the movies one time, when they were about in the sixth grade, and Mr. Conn, Russ Conn, a very good watercolor artist, insisted that their Negro maid go along as a chaperone for these two kids, and because the maid was with them, they had to sit up in the balcony. I never knew it when I was a kid.

A lot of kids went swimming in the basin. I don't know if I should tell you this, but there was an area they called the "nigger" basin, and the black kids would swim there. That was back in the 1940s. I never liked that term.

Another thing I never knew was that some of the soda fountains in the town were segregated. A few years back a fellow who was on the Boonton High School football team in the late 1940s told me that after a football game everybody said, "Let's go to Worman's," which was a local soda fountain. After the war, Mr. Worman opened up a liquor store because his customers had grown up. [Laughs.] Anyway, this fellow said that after the game the guys . . . used to go to Worman's because that's where all the girls went, and they had an ice-cream soda fountain there. Elmer Sims, the quarterback of the team, was a black kid, and they wouldn't let Elmer into Worman's. So a couple of guys from the team would go up to my dad's store. Elmer could come up there anytime.

—Lloyd Charlton

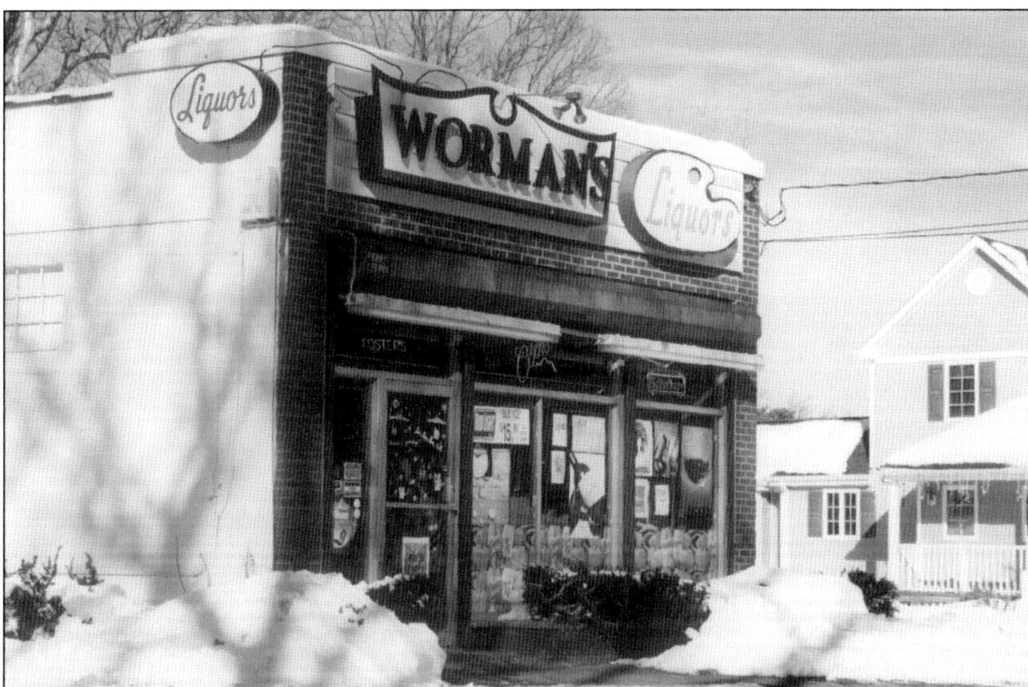

Worman's liquor store.

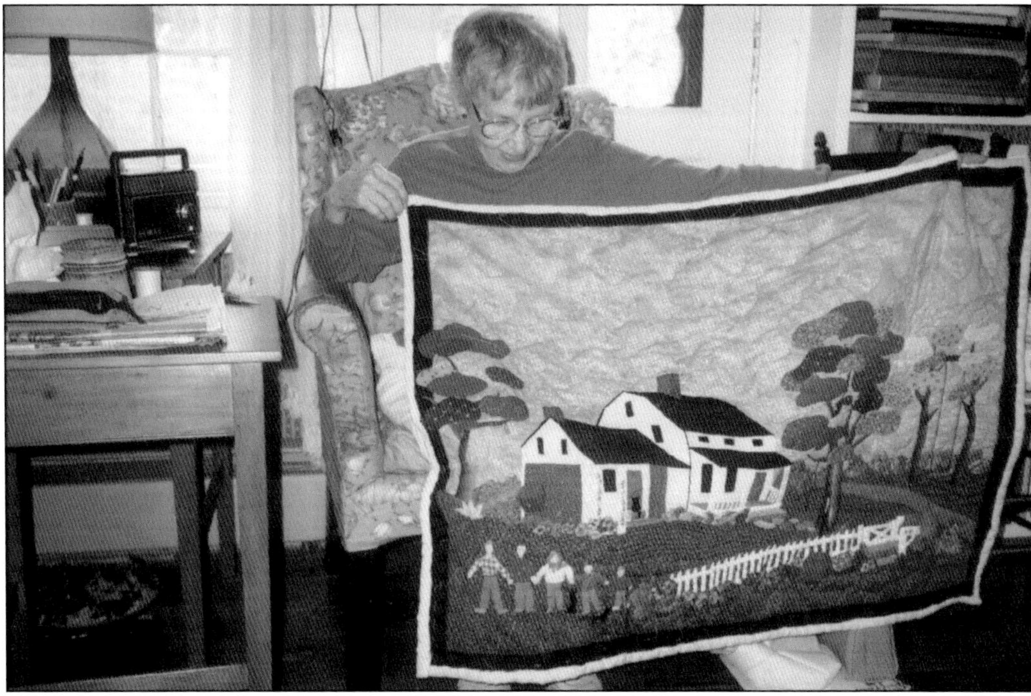

Merk Fowler displaying one of her attractive, early American quilts.

I had not had a full-time job since I was married. I taught for a couple of years before I was married, but I was not able to get a New Jersey teacher's license. So I became a substitute teacher for a couple of years. That's a terrible job, a terrible job. [Laughs.] The kids are lying in wait for substitute teachers. And if a substitute teacher has a southern accent, that makes for a very long day. [Laughs.] They imitated my accent back at me.

I was always a good teacher one on one, but I never got to be a really good disciplinarian. A lot of people still think I have a very strong southern accent. And when I go down south they say, "You talk like a Yankee." [Laughs.]

—Merk Fowler

My husband, Charles Henry, or "Slim" as everyone called him, was the greatest looking thing that ever came down the pike. [Laughs.] In Ireland, his father was the second son in the family, so he couldn't inherit the family property. Here, he designed those vests for that famous men's store, Rogers Peet.

You know he walked across the Hudson River over the ice in the winter. My grandfather walked across the East River. You know who Malcolm Forbes was? Well, his father invited the chief of the cops, I think in Bernardsville, to get some of his men and join them on his yacht. We went up and down the Hudson River and inland.

Everyone was down below drinking, and I'm sitting with the captain above in the pilot's house, enjoying the Palisades. When you came to the place where you go back into the Hudson at Spuyten Duyvil, there's the George Washington Bridge with the sun setting.

I'm 83 years old and I can still see it today in my mind. What the hell—I would never be able to do that again. Neither would the rest of them, but they were down below filling their guts.

—Doris McCoy

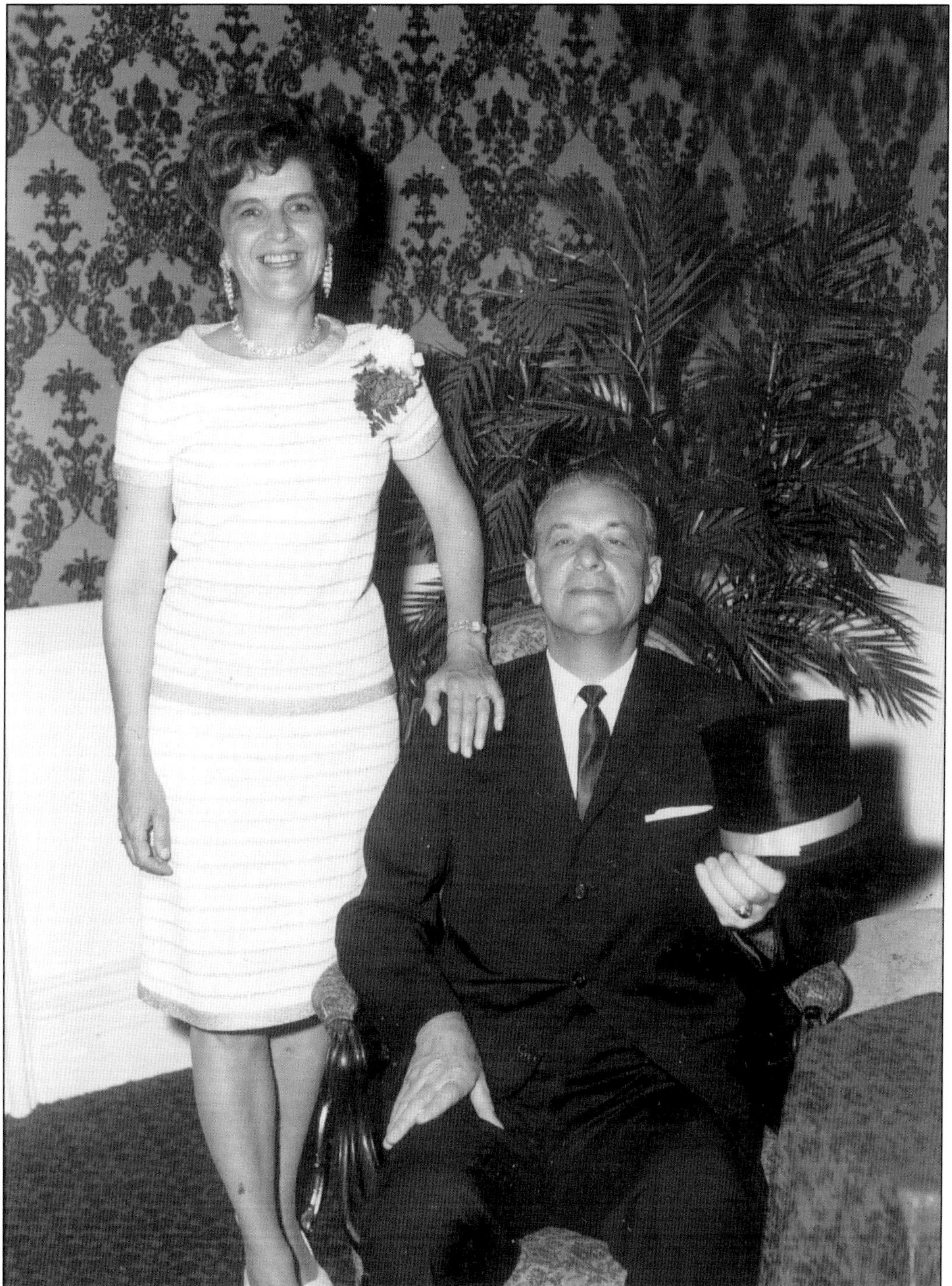

Doris and Charles Henry McCoy during the centennial celebrations.

It was much too late that I had the job of making the acquaintance of "Frenchy." I'd seen him around and heard of him for years but I only came to know him toward the end of his life. We met in a tavern where twice a week he would wait for a ride home for his chores of teaching piano or violin.

He was one of the most interesting men I've met. There was a time, he told me, "I was playing for the Philharmonic in Chicago. I was returning to my hotel this very cold night when dis man wass in front of me wiz a gun 'Geeve me your money.' he tol' me. I said, 'Wait a minute' and reached in my pocket. I also had a gun. I took it out and shot heem."

I asked if he called the police or anything. "No! I went to my hotel. I told nobody. The son of a beetch wanted to steal my money. I went to bed and went to sleep."

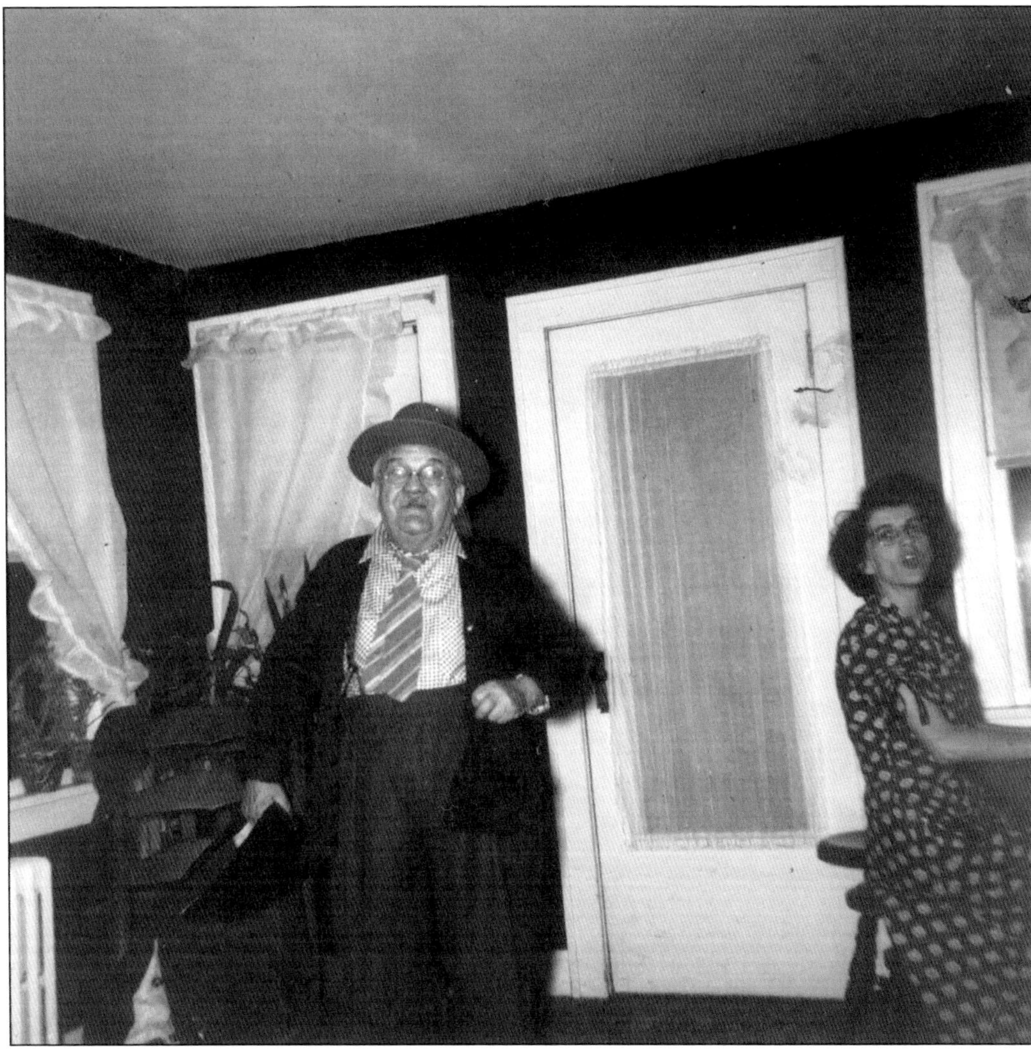

A musical evening with "Frenchy" singing and Doris McCoy at the piano, spring 1956.

What little I managed to learn from "Frenchy" was that his name was Lucien DeGazou and that he probably had an upper-middle-class rearing. He once told me that as a child he was introduced to Victor Hugo and Guy de Maupassant.

He told me he had played trumpet for the New York Philharmonic. Then, when the musicians decided to organize a union, Frenchy quit. He would be a free agent and take jobs as they came.

At some point they sent him to Boonton to play piano accompaniment to the silent movies at the Lyceum. After hearing him they offered him a steady job.

"Tell me," he once asked, "Ees zair any good feeshing around here?"

"Wonderful fishing!" he was told and they pointed him to the river.

Later he told me, "I feeshed there wahn afternoon and I sent a telegram to my wife in Chicago. 'Marie—Quit your job—We're moving to Boonton.'" And they did.

Frenchy taught trumpet, violin, and piano and played for the silent movies at the Lyceum, while mischievous boys pelted him with candies during the chase scenes. He loved Boonton and he loved to fish.

—Jim Monaghan

Frenchy was the town character and a cute, old fellow. Mother had a store in Boonton on Main Street, and we had a boxer named Squire. He was a wonderful dog. But he hated Frenchy with a passion. Squire hated any man who came around with a cap. You had a cap, you were in deep trouble.

One time a repairman came around to fix the refrigerator. This man had a very high voice and he had gone underneath the refrigerator to fix something. Well, when he came out he made one sound to start speaking. The dog attacked him and bit him on the nose.

One day Frenchy came by Mother's store. She had just rearranged the showroom. Everything looked very nice and Frenchy came sauntering by. The dog is sitting there. He always sat in the window and looked at the people passing by. He'd be like a statue and when the people would pass by just his head would move. But when he saw Frenchy he went berserk. And, oh my God, he was snarling and foaming at the mouth, and Frenchy was on the outside with his little beret and fishing rod and laughing, "Ho ho ho!" He thought Squire was so funny.

Mom loved the dog. She took Squire for a walk on Main Street. They came to "Henrietta's Deli," long since gone. The Bond bread man came in his van. He had a cap on. Squire went right through the screen of the van. The Bond man was holding this wooden tray with all his bread in it. The bread went flying, the guy fled into the back of the truck, and Mother is shouting, "Oh, he won't hurt you. He won't hurt you." And the guy is warding the dog off with his newspaper.

Once [Frenchy] had an argument with his wife. He came to see Mother and said, "You know, I haven't spoken to my wife for months. And one night she came up to the bedroom wearing her night dress and carrying a candle, looking all around in the closet, under the bed, in the drawers. Finally, I had to say, 'What are you looking for?' And she said to me, 'Your tongue.'"

—Corita Forrest

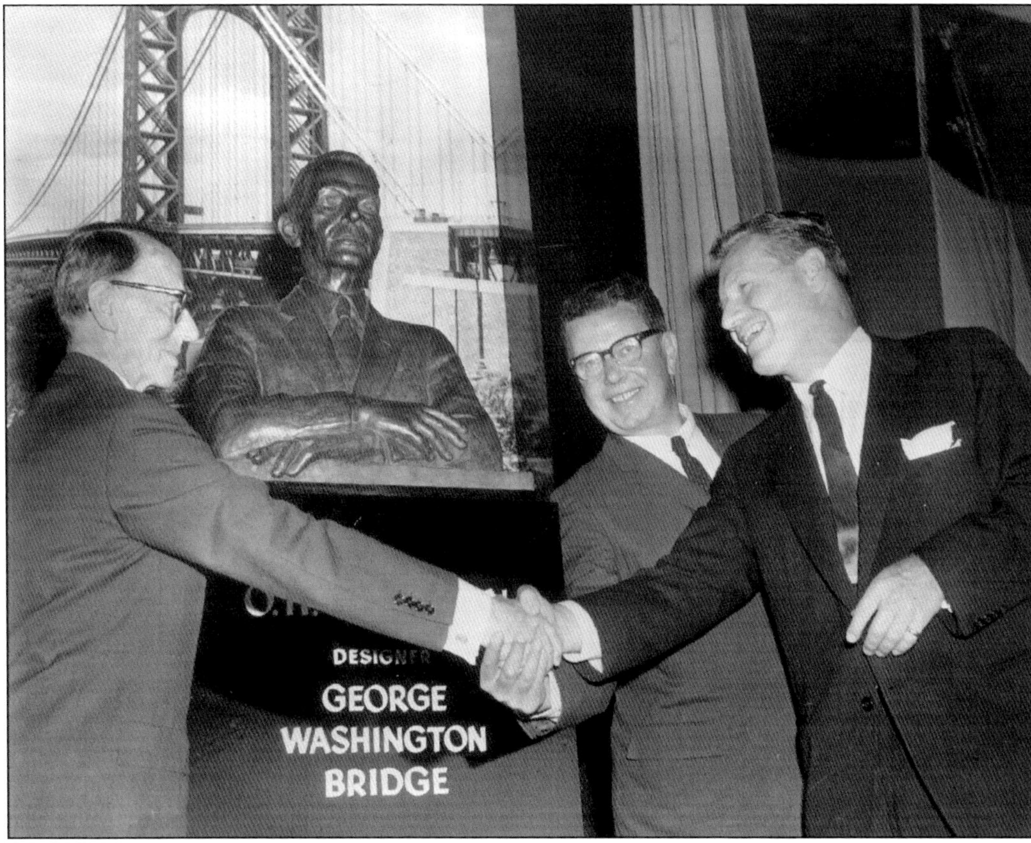

Othmar Ammann shaking hands with New York governor Nelson Rockefeller and Howard Hughes at the dedication ceremony for the opening of the second deck of the George Washington Bridge.

New York's Other Master Bridge Builder

Othmar Ammann's Name Is Largely Forgotten, but His Mighty and Graceful Creations Are His Enduring Legacy
by Bernard Stamler

His works soar above the water, spanning the city's rivers and connecting New York to the rest of the country. But who has heard of Othmar H. Ammann?

Donald Trump hadn't, at least not back in 1964 when he was a high school student and his father took him to the dedication ceremony for the Verrazano-Narrows Bridge.

"It was a sad experience," Mr. Trump recalled. "For years various politicians had fought the bridge. Now that it was built, I watched as these same people all got up and took credit for it, congratulating themselves and introducing one another. The only one not introduced was the man who made the bridge, Othmar Ammann.

"I had to ask who he was," Mr. Trump said. "I didn't know who he was, either."

Ammann (1879–1965), designer and builder of many of the city's great long-span bridges, is far less well known than New York's most famous bridge builder, John Augustus Roebling, the man behind the Brooklyn Bridge. But Amman was as much a molder of present-day New York as Roebling and even Robert Moses, the master builder who was among Amman's greatest patrons.

In the 1920's and early 30's, when Amman was appointed as chief engineer for the Port of New York Authority, as it was then known, and the Triborough Bridge and Tunnel Authority, and later, as a sought-after consultant, he was responsible for building the city's great 20th-century spans: the George Washington Bridge (1931), the Bayonne (1931), Triborough (1936), Bronx-Whitestone (1939), Throgs Neck (1961) and Verrazano-Narrows. A peerless manager, he also supervised the construction of the Lincoln Tunnel and consulted on other projects in New York and beyond, including the Golden Gate Bridge in San Francisco.

"No civil engineer gave more bridges to a single city than Amman did to New York" wrote Darl Rastorfer, the author of *Six Bridges: The Legacy of Othmar H. Ammann*. . . .

But it is not so surprising that others, notably Moses, held the public's attention during this era, for Amman was notable for his supremely modest and self-effacing personality.

A Swiss immigrant who came to America in 1904 at age 25, Amman lived for most of his career in Boonton, N.J. and as Rastorfer, put it, "he just got elbowed out of the way" by the "big egos" in the big city. Mr. Amman's design skills were widely recognized. His countryman Le Corbusier called the George Washington "the most beautiful bridge in the world . . . the only seat of grace in the disordered city."

When the Verrazano opened in 1964, its creator was 85. About a year later, in an interview shortly before his death, he was asked the source of his success. As was typical, he responded modestly. He had been "lucky," he said. "Lucky."

—From the *New York Times*, Sunday, April 16, 2000

Reunion of BHS Class of 1939
August 27, 1994

Well, hello fellow classmates! It's great to see you all again and celebrate 55 years of survival since graduation from BHS.

I thought you might like to remember the changes we have all witnessed in these years. It's a bit mind-boggling.

We were born before frozen foods and instant coffee, before penicillin and polio shots, copy machines, faxing, cellular phones, plastics and the pill.

We didn't know of radar, credit cards, split atoms, laser beams and ball-point pens. We were before panty-hose, dishwashers, electric blankets, air conditioners, drip dry clothing and before man walked on the moon, or suitcases were on wheels.

In our time, closets were for clothes, not for "coming out of". Bunnies were small rabbits and rabbits were not Volkswagens. Having a meaningful relationship meant getting along with our cousins. We thought fast food was what you ate during Lent.

We never heard of FM radios, tape decks, electric typewriters, artificial hearts, computers, yoghurt, and guys wearing earrings. For us time sharing meant togetherness, not condominiums. A chip was something off the old block, hardware was hardware, and software wasn't even a word.

We hit the scene when there were 5 and 10¢ stores where you bought things for 5 and 10¢. Ice cream cones sold for a nickel or a dime. For one nickel you could ride a streetcar, make a phone call, buy a Pepsi or enough stamps to mail one letter and two postcards. You could buy a new Chevy Coupe for $600, but who could afford one? A real pity, because gas was 11¢ a gallon. Milk was 12¢ a quart, eggs 39¢ a dozen, pants $4.50 a pair and a one carat diamond ring cost $365.

In our day cigarette smoking was fashionable, grass was mowed, Coke was a drink, and pot was something you cooked in. Rock music was grandma's lullaby and aids were helpers in the principal's office.

We certainly knew the difference between the sexes, but we were surely before the sex change. We made do with what we had, and we were the last generation that was so dumb as to think a woman needed a husband to have a baby.

Now wonder we are so confused!

We went to "Gone with the Wind" and whistled "Over the Rainbow". Franklin D. Roosevelt was our president.

It began raining in the middle of our graduation ceremony but we went on with the program. Our guests put up their umbrellas. We've been going on ever since then.

So let's forget our arthritis and our hearing aids and our cataracts and celebrate our survival. We've made it so far, we will make it the rest of the way!

—Margot Ammann, *Remembering those Boonton Years*,
55th Reunion Class of 1939, August 27, 1994

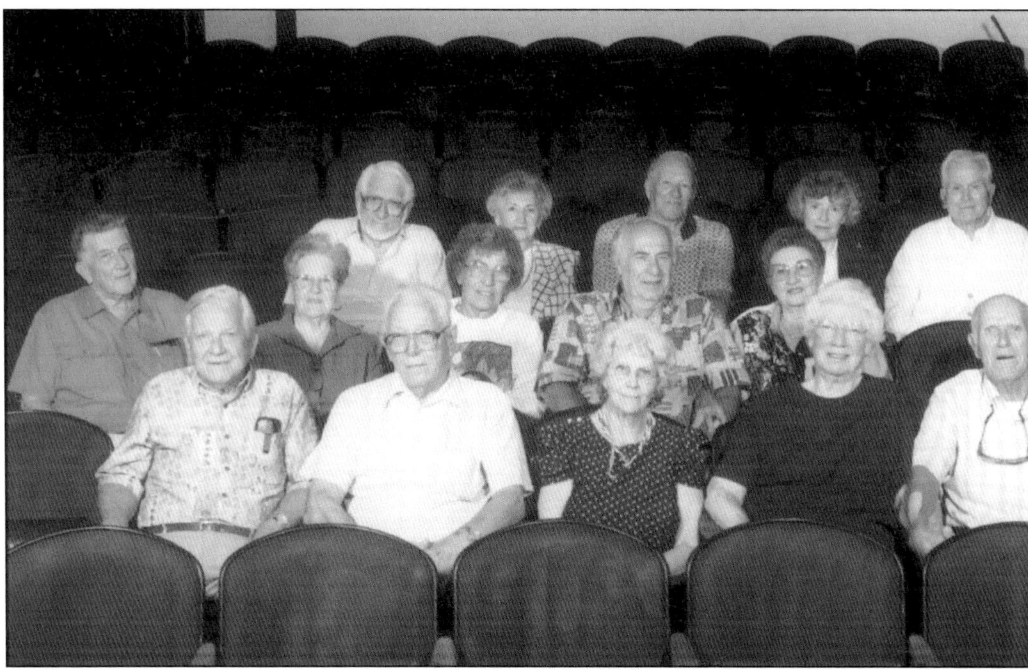

A photograph of a Boonton 60th class reunion, taken at the State Theater, September 1999. From left to right are the following: (front row) Dr. William Sikora, Henry Popovich, Arline Fowler Dempsey, Alma Conn Hallock, and Henry Levitski; (middle row) Warren Brush, Dorothy Mackallor Brush, Marion Levitski, Remy Baker, and Elizabeth Higgs Baker; (back row) Larry Rea, Mary Falduto, Ralph Lucas, Elizabeth Black Hardy, and Morgan Hardy.

Chapter Seven
World War II

In the army I was an ammunition technician. I passed out ammunition to all the different outfits. We were supposed to hit Normandy the first day. There were thousands and thousands of soldiers on the coast of Wales. "We're moving out," they said. We didn't know where we were going, but we came to the port where the boats were. We got on the boat and went out into the [English] Channel overnight. The next morning we set out, but we were hit by a mine. The ship was sinking. We had to get off and scramble onto anything we could that would pick [us] up. Those boats, they go on water and land, we called them "ducks." They could get you so close to the shore and then the front would drop down, and we would pile out. Later we heard those boats made a success of the invasion. All we knew is that we had to jump out and run for our lives.

You can't visualize, you know what I mean, bodies floating all over, men being killed to the right and left of you . . . wonder why you are alive. We scrambled up on the beach.

Nobody had to tell you what to do. You just had to run anywhere with the shells falling all around you. You didn't know which way to go.

—John Curran

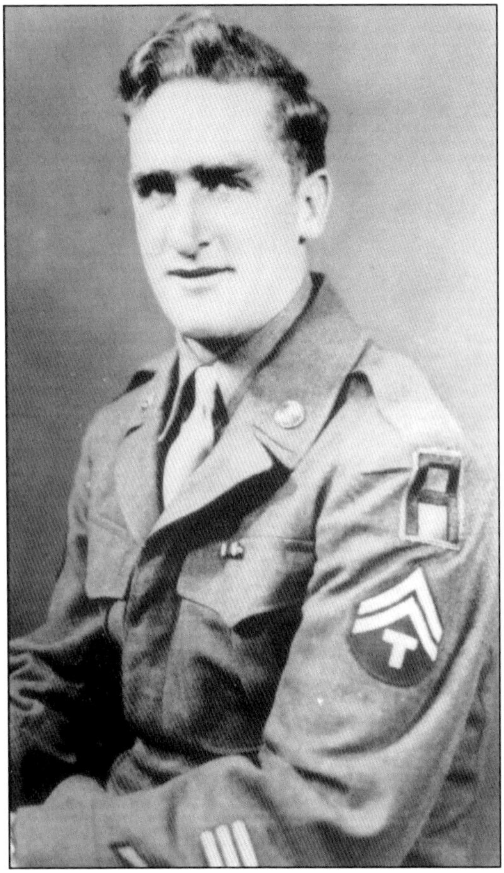

John Curran, 1944.

I was stationed in Italy. When we came back to the rear areas for rest, and then, of course, we had hot meals, but we never had a garbage can in our outfit. It was there, but we didn't use it. You know the reason why? The civilians in the area had nothing. They had money, but they couldn't buy anything. There were no stores, there was nothing. We supplied them with our leftover food. They'd come around and wait for it. Women, young girls with small babies would come in, get some formula for their babies, because we always had evaporated milk. The cooks used it. I tell you, it was a sad thing to see that people would go hungry if it wasn't for us being there. I was in the medics and they knew they could come in on sick call. Nobody would bother them. If we could help them, we would.

Back in the headquarters these two fellows came for a rest. Afterward, the officer sent them back to the line and one said, "I can't go back."

"Why not" the officer said, "You're all right now. You've gotta go back." You know what they did. They went across the street and shot themselves in the head.

Their chances of staying alive were just as good as ours. And we medics had no weapons. But they did. They had the advantage over us, really.

Lots of times in the field while we were on the front, anybody that wanted to surrender would surrender to us because they knew they wouldn't get shot. These two guys were married, with families back home. Why they chose to take that way out, I don't know. Well, that's the way of the world, I guess. If you can't take it . . . well, if we all felt that way we wouldn't have won the war.

The 24th of September, 1944, was the day I got my purple heart. The 17th was the day we were ambushed. I had to take care of these two fellows and take them to another aid station, but after it got dark we didn't know where [the station] was. We went up after a casualty. Of course the Germans always had the high ground. They were lucky in that way—the lay of the land. We got halfway up the hill and then came the machine-gun fire. Every fifth round was a tracer, and where the tracers crossed was where they threw the 88s, mortar shells. They came piling in faster than I could count. The fellow who went before me was our sergeant, who went with us that day. He should have stayed in the aid station; that was his job. But he didn't.

We were short of men that day, and he volunteered to go with us. Then all of a sudden things quieted down a bit. So he went and stood up and I shouted, "Jack, don't stand up. You're going to get it." Well, he lived long enough to get to our aid station, where he died.

Afterward you are left with the memories of the fellows you trained with, went through the whole damn war with, and you wonder when you got home, why is it that you made it and a lot of your buddies didn't. Our particular unit was 20 men, all medics, including two officers. I think that out of our outfit there were only about four of us who survived to the end.

—Larry Dixon

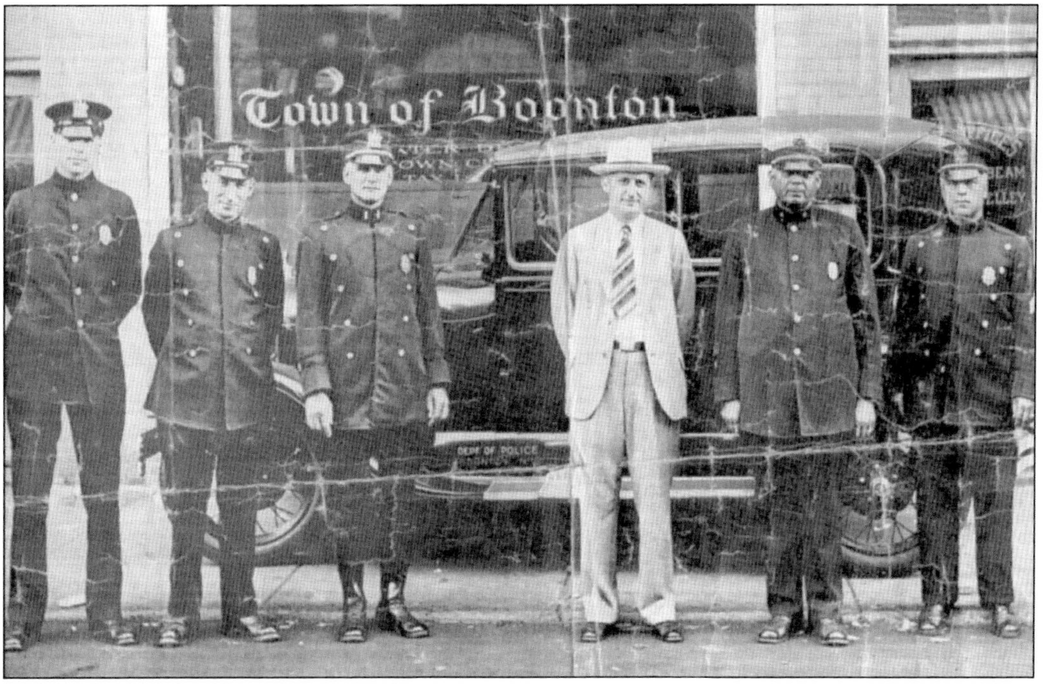

The Boonton Police Department. From left to right are Charles McCoy and John Conn (patrolmen), William Lucas (lieutenant), Herbert L. Dixon (commissioner), Eli Vanderhoof (chief), and Frank Kromka (sergeant).

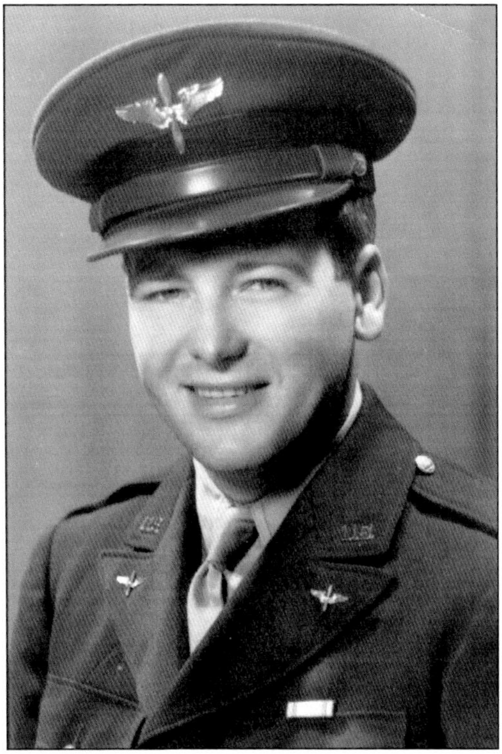

Albert Mitchko, youngest brother of Bill Mitchko.

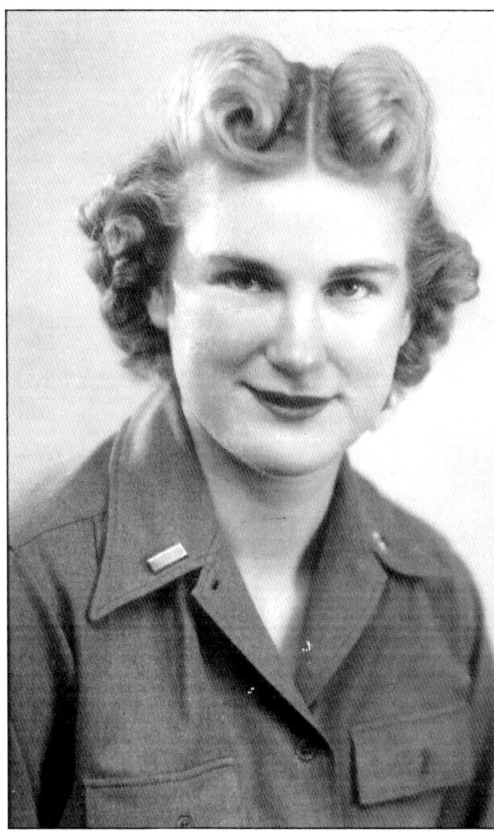

Capt. Jane Hopkins, awarded the Bronze Star.

My brother was 19 years old when he got in the army. He wanted to get into the air force but he was very near-sighted. Anyway, he was a hell of a musician. He could play almost any instrument, so when he got drafted they assigned him to entertaining the troops. He organized a band and he'd work almost every night entertaining the officers. But later on they gave him an eye examination and found out that he could perceive distance very well, and that a near-sighted man had good vision to pinpoint areas for bombing. They took him right out of the entertainment unit and put him in the air corps. For about six months he was trained to fly an airplane.

When he flew his 12th mission he was supposed to get two days rest, but he was a spunky kid and he volunteered for a 13th mission. That's when he got shot down in the Romanian oil fields.

When they were hit he ordered his two gunners to bail out, shouting, "I'm hit!" With that they bailed out. As soon as they did he smashed into the side of a mountain.

My mother wanted his body to be sent home. But an officer came to my mother and said, "Mrs. Mitchko, don't pay the air force $600 to have him sent home, because you're not going to get anything. They're only going to send you an empty box."

—Bill Mitchko

In 1941, I decided to go into the army. I had just finished my nurse's training. Twenty-one days after D-Day we were on Omaha Beach. We set up a field hospital and we went all across Europe. Our first base was at St. Marie Eglise. Our patients had either to be chest or belly and couldn't travel. Then we had a 24-hour surgical team that worked with us. On August 7, the Germans retook the town of Mortain. The 30th Division suffered heavy casualties, and many of them couldn't be rescued because German armor fanned out beyond the town. At our hospital the casualties mounted. The Third Auxers tried to keep up, but the backlog had mounted to 16 patients. One of the nurses from the postoperative ward rushed in, wiping blood from her neck. The operating tent was shot through in a dozen places. The patients were becoming hysterical. At the front a man could at least have found cover. Here he was defenseless. We lost a lot of people there and it had been a really bad night.

The next morning I walked out of the tent just to relax, and I heard these church bells. I was looking across to the next field and I could see our infantry crawling up the hill toward us and I thought, God, I may really be in a war this time. [Laughs.] And when the bombing started, I jumped into the foxhole. [Laughs.] That's when I got my medal [the Bronze Star].

—Jane Hopkins

I wanted to go into the navy, but they wouldn't take me because I was underweight. Anyway, I volunteered in the old firehouse on Main Street on June 6, 1941, and I was discharged October 6, 1941. On the bulletin board during my basic training in Camp Edwards, Massachusetts, there was a notice asking for anyone that wanted to volunteer for . . . the Army Air Force. With only a one-year high school education I passed for pilot and bombardier training. I graduated as an aerial gunner.

When we arrived in England they indoctrinated us by having us fly around England to look over the different landmarks when you come into a base. In case they would be hit we would still recognize them. A few days passed, and we were doing no flying and we were itching to go. Not that we were gung-ho.

Anyway, my pilot was sent to Greencastle, Ireland. He was going to go there with his B-24. And two other planes were going to go over with him. In one of the airplanes was nine personnel and in the other was ten. And those two airplanes were going to be left there and salvaged. If somebody needed the usable parts, they would come over and get them. That morning the crew chief said to me, "Steve, how would you like to see where your stepmother came from in Ireland?" "Sure," I said, "that would be great." It was about 7:30 in the morning. "I'll see you at the mess hall." I turned over and fell asleep, I got up at 10:30 and they had left without me.

At about a quarter to three, Capt. Leo Cook came in. He was carrying those mattress covers where they put all your belongings in when something happened. And I said, "What happened, sir?" And he said, "Oh, my God. We lost 24 men." I just felt the whole world drop.

Well, coming back to England, one of those planes exploded. It killed 24 men. And those 19 men had completed 35 missions. All they were waiting for was stateside papers to bring them home. If I hadn't overslept I wouldn't be talking to you today.

—Stephen Bolcar

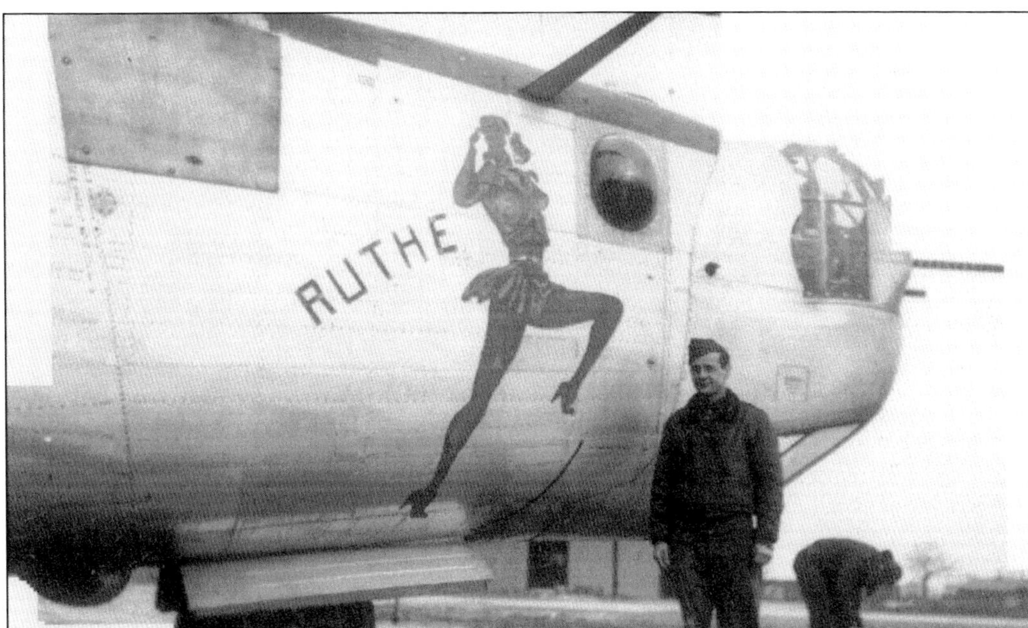

S.Sgt. Stephen Bolcar standing by his B-24 Liberator.

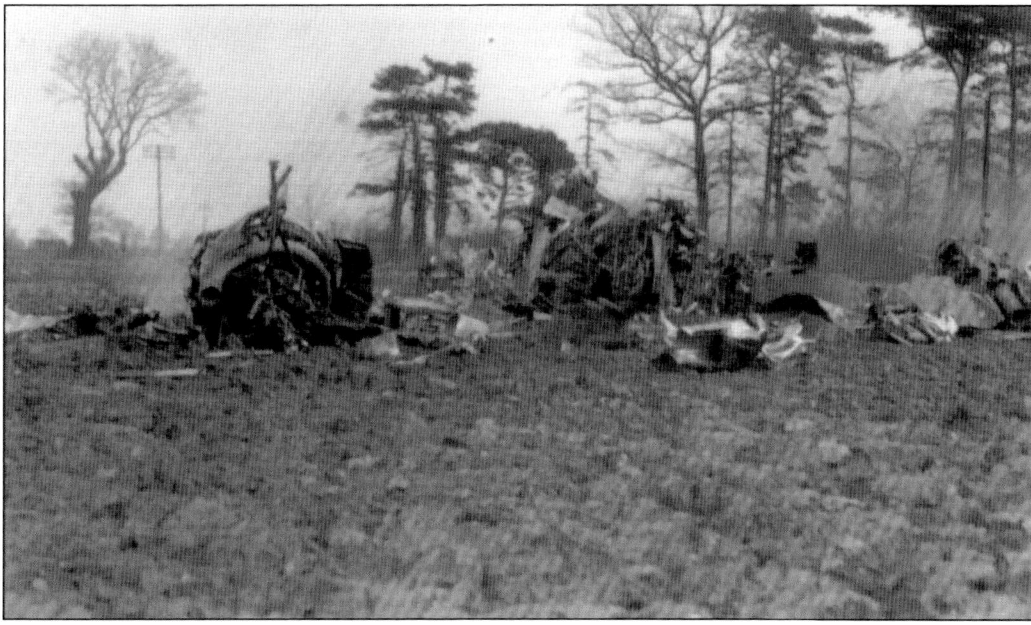

Crash landing kills 24 USAAF personnel at Landican near Liverpool, England, on October 18, 1944.

British Honor 24 from the 445th BG Killed in Crash near Liverpool

The dedication of a memorial commemorating 24 USAAF personnel who died when their B-24 Liberator crashed at Landican on 18 October 1944 was held on Saturday, September 1996 at Wirral, CIIr. The crash report states that this aircraft, a B-24 Liberator assigned to the 445th Bomb Group, was on a return journey with air crews from repair depot Greencastle, Northern Ireland, to its home base at Tibenham, Norfolk, via North Wales.

—Submitted by Ralph G. Scott, Secretary, Bad 2 Association

When the war was going on in Ethiopia before I joined the service and all the Italians were going over to fight, there was a song, "Viva Italia," that I learned on the radio. It's when Italy was building up its army and Mussolini sent a squadron of planes to New York to show how far ahead they were in aviation. I think they called them the black shirts, and they wanted volunteers. But those people were worse than Hitler's bunch. My father said, "Why don't you go over there?" And I said, "Hell no, I don't want to go over there." I really don't think he really wanted me to go in the first place, to tell you the truth.

I had been working at the Boonton Molding Company when I joined the service in 1940. I joined in Morristown. I was young and I guess you could say that I wanted adventure. I wanted to join up for the Philippines and asked to go overseas, but they sent me to Panama. I spent two years down there. And then on December 7, 1941, when the war broke out, we moved out to the West Indies, to Trinidad, and stayed there a year. As we were coming back to the States we stopped off in Puerto Rico, where they were asking for volunteers for a certain unit. We had no idea where we were going or what we would be doing. We found out we were going to India to form a certain unit to fight in Burma. We were the first American troops to fight in Asia. We called ourselves the "Fifty-three-o-seven

Composite Unit." We didn't even know that we were called "Merrill's Marauders" until we were halfway through the campaign.

When we first got our mules we heard their tongues were going to be cut out to keep them from making noise and alerting the enemy, but then the decision was made that, "What the hell, the Japs know we're here so why do that?" When I got dysentery and malaria so bad, they wanted me to ride a mule but I was too weak to stay on it, so I held on to its tail and he pulled me up and down hills, letting out wind most of the way.

The Japanese had one lone artilleryman, and he would fire at the same time every day. We called him "Pistol Pete." He got some of our mules, who then polluted the water. So we had to have water dropped into our perimeter, but half of our supplies fell outside the perimeter and we couldn't get to them. They dropped water and plastic bags of food with fried chicken and bread, and that's the first decent meal we'd had in a long time. On Easter Sunday 1944, the 3rd and 1st Battalions got us out.

We had a certain mission to accomplish, to get this airstrip in middle Burma at Myitkyina, so we could bring in troops and supplies. I was with the Blue Combat I & R (Intelligence and Reconnaissance) Platoon and was on the first patrol to have a firefight with the enemy, where the first man in Merrill's Marauders was killed. There were five of us on that patrol. After the firefight I saw Sergeant Cobb. He had lost his helmet and rifle. He was crying and said, "They got Landis," who was the youngest on the patrol. That was the first time I'd been under enemy fire.

When we finally reached our objective, the airstrip at Myitkyina, we had traveled over 500 miles by foot to our destination. They sent in the 475th as replacements for some of the original Merrill's Marauders who had malaria, typhus, and dysentery. In July, I left for the States. I still have my "short snorter," which is a dollar bill with all my buddies' names on it. I went all the way through World War II with Merrill's Marauders and didn't get injured. But after I came back to the States at Camp Wheeler, we were training with mines and booby traps, using a quarter stick of dynamite, and someone tripped a wire and it caught me and another guy. I was in the hospital with two punctured eardrums, blinded, and my right hand was split open. I got out with a 50 percent disability and moved to Knoxville, Tennessee, where I worked at Alcoa for a while. And then I returned to the service. I was married and had a family at that time, and we were all living in Hawaii, when I was shipped off to the Korean War.

I was wounded in Korea when an artillery shell went off and split open my nose, but it wasn't too bad, so I went back into action. Soon after that, they started sending some of us home on points. That's when I came home, flying into Knoxville, Tennessee. I was one of the first GIs back from the Korean War. Everyone was there taking pictures, and it was in the news all over the place.

—Vincent Melillo

My father was working for Curtis-Wright during World War II, and this German fellow was constantly stopping production. I mean he'd throw a pen or a pencil or a wrench into these vats. He was always doing something to stop production, daily. My father thought there was something going on there. You can do it once or twice, but this was happening every day. So my father went to the FBI. And he said to my mother, "Marie, the FBI may be coming to see me. Don't get upset." So one Saturday the doorbell rings and this man is standing there. And my mother says, "Oh, you must be from the FBI." And he says, "Oh, does it show?" [Laughs.] Anyway, my father and he sat down and started talking, and on Monday the personnel manager came and took this fellow right off the line. Nobody ever saw him again.

—Corita Forrest

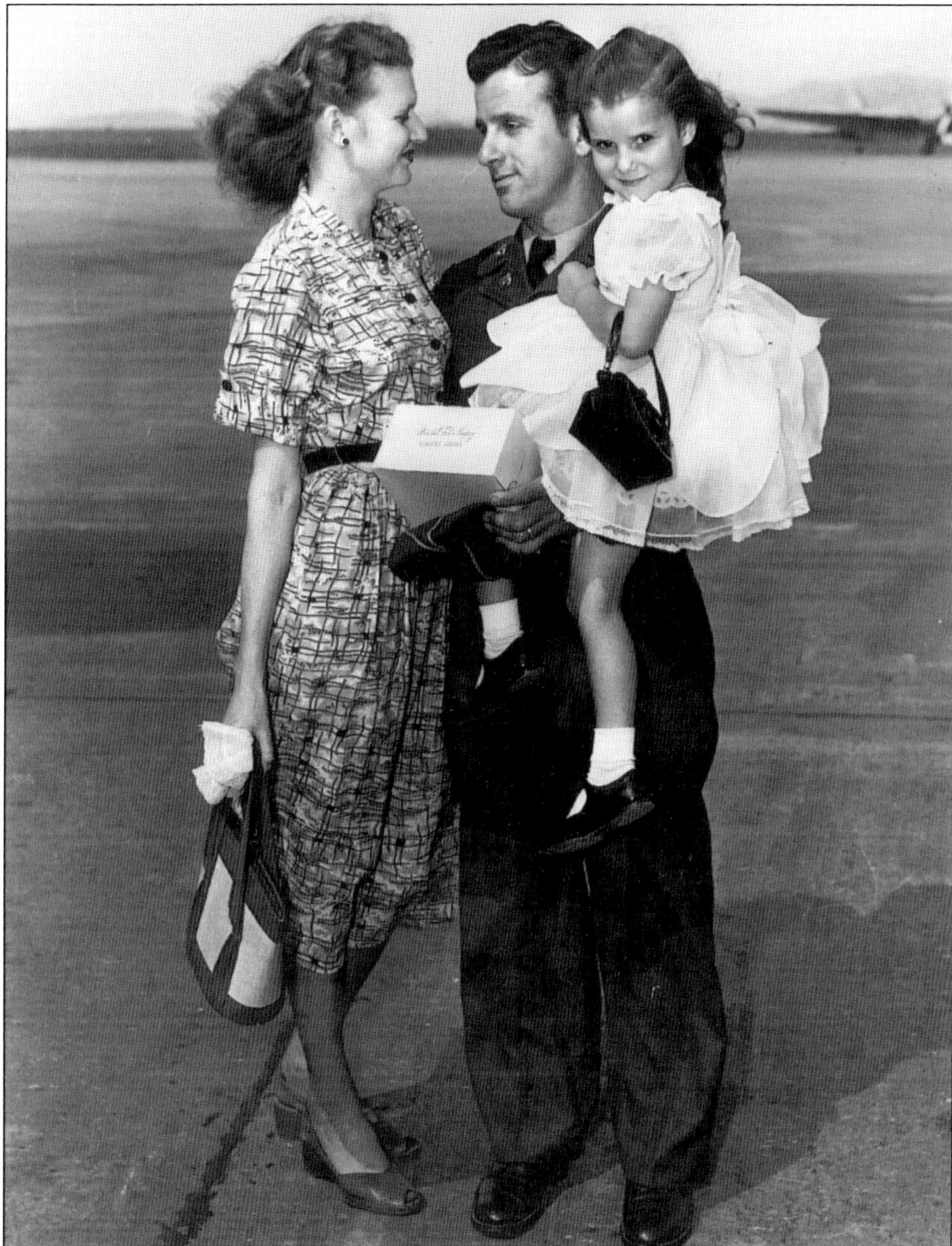

Vincent Melillo greets his wife, Frankie, and daughter Jonnie in Knoxville, Tennessee, when he was the first soldier to return to Knoxville from the Korean War.

Boonton Military Service Committee
Vol. 5, no. 6, August 2000

In a recent issue I talked about this group, which kept in touch with Boonton service people during World War II. In a recent collection of material given the Historical Society by the American Legion is the August 14, 1943 copy of *Liberty* magazine, carrying a full-page story called "Boonton Remembers Them."

Among the subjects covered were a 1938 debate on birth control between Margaret Sanger and Mahatma Ghandi, and a discussion on the threat of war by Charles De Gaulle and Neville Chamberlain. Articles in this issue included features about Americans of Japanese descent who were sent to relocation camps during World War II and another about U.S. and Canadian attacks on German U-Boats on the North Atlantic Route. Boonton's extraordinary concern for its service men and women was accorded a prominent place among these other significant social and cultural questions during the early and mid-twentieth century.

According to the article, "The organization was founded in November, 1940, when Marziale Robibero, an Italian paint-store owner . . . remembered his induction day, leaving for the Army without so much as a 'So long, and good luck' from somebody he knew. He remembered the long days at the front without mail, the Christmas without a gift. And he remembered his homecoming—arriving back in Boonton in 1920 with only a few dollars in his pocket and no job, no civilian clothes, no home, no place to sleep."

Robibero contacted the Gus Ginder Post No. 242, VFW, to ask that something be done for local boys going into the current war. With their help, twenty-seven town organizations, each pledging seventeen dollars a year, became the Boonton Services Committee, sending Boonton Times subscriptions, Christmas and birthday gifts, and helping the service men and women and their families with problems. The Board of Aldermen earmarked $10,000 for such postwar projects.

—From "Nosy PARKer," vol. 5, no. 6, August 2000

Just before we got married my husband was a resident in Butler, New Jersey. I was from New York. We were engaged and planning to get married, and he bought a business in Boonton. He was in the service during the war. We met at a Broadway show. I was with a girl friend and he was with another soldier. They were stationed at Camp Shanks in Orangeburg. When he got out he thought he would look for a business and he found it in Boonton. I just went along with it. A young girl gets married and you go where your husband goes.

My first recollection of Boonton was that I was in a Midwest town. It looked like a place you saw in the movies. I could picture tying a horse to where Whelan's drugstore was, where the post office is now. There were all these hills, but that didn't bother me, because I came from the Bronx where there were lots of hills too. There were also trolley car tracks there in 1946. My husband liked New Jersey. He was a country boy. That was his home. His family had a clothing store in Butler. We were in Boonton for three months and then we had a big fire . . . in 1947. We stood right there and watched it burn. Two buildings on either side of us also burned down. So it wasn't a very good start.

—Laurie Goldberg

The business was a ladies' and children's shop. The original store was a small shop, nothing like what it became. And after the fire we were out of work, out of business, and out of money. So we looked around for another store. Eventually we rented another store, next door to Heavenly Coffee. Then we had to start all over again.

We stayed in that second store until 1958. Then we had the opportunity to buy the building next to the movies.

—Nathan Goldberg

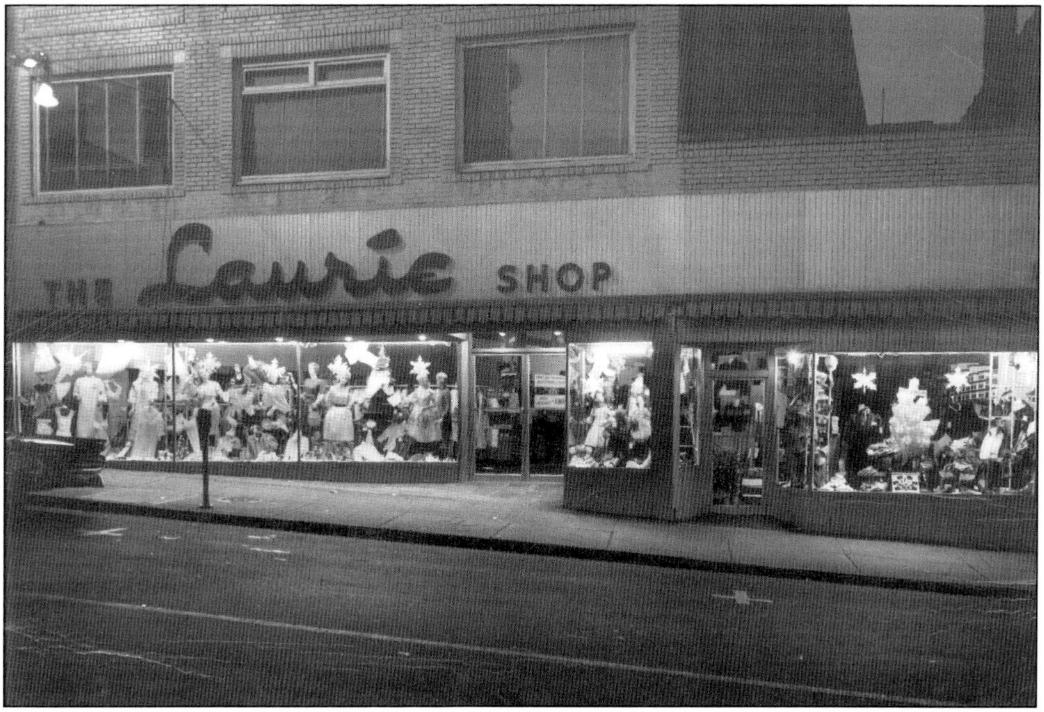

The Laurie Shop, Main Street.

Friday night was a big night for shopping in Boonton. Lots of the movie crowd used to come in. They would come in from Lake Hiawatha, Montville, and Towaco, because Boonton was the center of everything. The other towns didn't have banks. And Friday night was bank night. Everybody came to do their banking and shopping, and go to the movies.

We liked Boonton right away. We made a lot of friends, we joined the temple. What was nice about the town and about business was that people shopped in their own town. We knew them, they knew your name, we knew their name, you knew how many children they had. You got to know their tastes, what they liked, what to show them.

Everybody charged. Our original customers charged on our books without interest. Later we got into Master[card] and Visa, but when we started it was all personal. It was a business of trust. Of course then we didn't have any malls.

Our third store was two floors, and then we went into men's clothing and boys' and household—it was a department store.

We had a store like Kohl's. We sold clothes for everybody, household, sheets, linen, tablecloths. We had a boy scout department. It just evolved into everything. Our store had an old-world charm.

People would come in around Christmas from the Midwest and they would say, "Oh, this store reminds me of one that we have in Georgia or Virginia." We had lots of stealing, break-ins, shoplifters. I had to get robbed four or five times before we got a burglar alarm. One time they stole thousands of Jordache jeans when they first came out. They were very popular. [Laughs.] The burglar alarm was hooked up to the police station, and in the middle of the night they would call us: "Mrs. Goldberg, you'd better come down at the store." We knew what that meant. The cops were all good. They always looked out for us.

We didn't quit until 1990. We were there for more than 40 years. When we first opened the kids wore shirts and ties, or uniforms if they went to parochial school. The girls would wear dresses. Women would wear skirts and blouses or jumpers, and then all of a sudden they started to wear slacks and then, of course, they went into dungarees. The men called them jeans. The hippies were a whole thing by themselves.

—Laurie Goldberg

The 1940s were the best years in Boonton, even though the war was on. They were beautiful years for us. I think the family structure was so strong then. There was hope that the war would end, and that we would win it. I had a brother in the service, and hoped that he would come home safe and sound.

—Edith Bohacik

At that time the entire Main Street was filled with stores and Friday night was the big night in town. And hosiery was the big money maker. In the 1940s, hosiery workers were making over $100 a week, so all the stores, the taverns, were humming all week long.

—Stephen Bohacik

Anything you needed was right there on Main Street. All kinds of shops, beautiful little shops.

—Edith Bohacik

The ice-cream stores were the big thing for the ladies and the children, and the taverns for the men. And the gathering place of the workers that frequented the taverns was Bevin's Diner. No matter where they were they'd wind up at Bevin's. Next door to it was the Lyceum [Theatre]. Generally in the evening the men would gather there on the stairs. And the center attraction was a fellow called Fonzie Aquilino, who would play a banjo and sing. Every evening in the summer you would see a group of fellows gathered around and Fonzie singing there. Fonzie was there after the war, in [19]45. And then we had the band that used to play in Grace Lord park.

—Stephen Bohacik

And my father and two brothers used to play in it.

—Edith Bohacik

We Remember

Fifty years ago most of our classmates were involved—in one way or other, at home or abroad—in WORLD WAR II. The battles have been well publicized. We will remember by the popular songs we sang between 1940 and 1945. It was a time when the non-war songs included tunes like "Amapola, That Pretty Little Poppy," "Those Cool and Limpid Green Eyes," "Chattanooga Choo-Choo," "Tangerine," "Laura—But She's Only a Dream," and "I'm Dreaming of a White Christmas."

We were patriotic, united and determined. Just like Kate Smith, we meant it when we belted out "God Bless America." WE REMEMBER PEARL HARBOR. "We did it before and we can do it again," reminded Eddie Cantor. We admired the chaplain who urged, "Praise the Lord and pass the ammunition!" "There's a star-spangled banner flying somewhere," we were assured and were advised to "Shout wherever you may be: 'I AM AN AMERICAN!'"

We applauded Spike Jones' vocal raspberry: "Sieg heil! (b-r-r-p) right in the Fuhrer's face." "Goodbye, Dear, I'll be back in a year," promised departing GI's before the time limit was extended. It would be a breeze, we thought. Only 12 days after Pearl Harbor, Tin Pan Alley published, "Goodbye, Mama. I'm off to Yokahama."

It wouldn't be that easy. Crippled planes would be "Coming in on a wing and a prayer." Money was needed "Any bonds today?" pleaded Irving Berlin. There was "The Sinking of the Reuben James" and "The Ballad of Rodger Young," an infantryman who gave his all in the Solomons. We were warned not to give away secrets. "A slip of the lip can sink a ship," counseled Duke Ellington.

But we knew victory was forthcoming. It was heralded by "Stars and Stripes on Iwo Jima Isle." "There'll be a hot time in the town of Berlin when the Yanks go marching in" to the "Victory Polka." It would be wonderful, sang Vaughan Monroe, "When the lights go on again all over the world."

There were songs for the GI's like "This is the Army, Mr. Jones, no private rooms or telephones" and "What do you do in the infantry?" The "Dogface Soldier" was paid $21 A DAY ONCE A MONTH and "At mail call today" was his big moment. Despite the worries of staying alive and healthy, the serviceman's main concern was the girl(s) back home. "From taps to reveille I dream of you," confessed Bing Crosby. "I left my heart at the Stagedoor Canteen," mourned the soldier or sailor. "Don't sit under the apple tree with anyone else but me" and "Wait for me, Baby!" he pleaded. "I'll be home for Christmas" he hoped because "You'd be so nice to come home to." He listened to "Gonna take a sentimental journey, sentimental journey home."

At home he was not forgotten although "Rosie, the riveter" had gone to work. Girls proclaimed "He's 1-A in the Army and A-1 in my heart." The home front was advised to "Say a prayer for the boys over there." Everyone at home dreaded getting "A soldier's last letter." A better postal arrangement would be to fulfill a young miss's hope that "I wish I could hide inside this letter." Girls urged GI sweethearts to be faithful while assuring them of their own fidelity. "I'll Walk Alone," promised the girls by V-Mail and if you are told differently, "Do nothing till you hear from me" because the truth is "I don't get around much anymore." The longing grew intense: "When the boys come home" and, more personal, "When my man comes home."

And suddenly it was over and they returned: "My guy's come back." "We'll gather lilacs now that you're home once more." "Kiss me once and kiss me twice and kiss me once again—it's been a long, long time."

Amen to that! It was.

—From *Remembering those Boonton Years*,
55th Reunion Class of 1939, August 27, 1994

We didn't have the violence that we have today. We didn't have the communications we have now. If two or more kids are killed in Columbine, we didn't know about it in those days. What we knew about was published in the *Morristown Daily Record,* the local newspaper. In fact we didn't get a television set here until the late 1950s when I was just getting out of high school. Partially because our mothers didn't want us to have them, but also because a television set cost $1,000 and when your father is making $5,000 a year, that was kind of a steep price to pay for entertainment. You also didn't have all the violence on television you have now, sensationalizing every trivial thing that happens. Now when you turn on the news, it's the "murder du jour."

In the American Legion Hall they had one of the first television sets in town. We [also] listened to the radio. "The Lone Ranger" was very popular. Or families got together and they told stories. It was the same stories over and over again. They got better and better with the telling. You learned a lot of history, family history, history of the town.

The town had a newspaper, the *Boonton Times-Bulletin,* came out either once or twice a week. There was no news in it. Just legal news and parties and things like that. But the real scandals and things that went on in the town, you found out about them on the grapevine—the barbershop, the post office.

My uncle Henry had this grocery store. What happened was the postman would come down and whatever was happening in the town he would relate it to Uncle Henry, and my uncle would relate it to everyone who came into the store. Something that would happen in town, within hours, it was all over town, and everybody knew about it. Most of it was never printed in the newspaper, but you always knew what was going on.

In 1947, I was seven years old, and the town was full of veterans. We played war games all the time. I can remember the John Wayne movies; *The Battle of Iwo Jima* came out. We dug trenches and pill boxes. That's something important that people don't realize. Growing up in those times were very risky times for everybody.

My father was young enough that he avoided the first world war. He was only 14 when that war ended and he was too old and had too many kids when World War II came around. But he saw all of this coming. There was one war after another.

Now in my time there was World War II, and I can remember when I was living in Elizabeth of the air raids and the blackouts. And then in the early 1950s the school kids were worried about atomic bombs, the cold war with Russia. We used to have to duck under our desks and cover our heads and protect ourselves from the atomic flash. And they even trained us for civil defense.

When I was in high school they sent me down to Paterson to train me for a couple of weekends to detect poison gas in the water system and use Geiger counters and radiation maps. This was [19]45, and in [19]47 I can remember the tremendous, long convoys going to Fort Drummond on summer maneuvers.

In 1950, the Korean War came along, and that scared me pretty good. I was 10 or 11 years old and they had kids in the high school, 15 and 16 years old, that belonged to the Farmer's Battalion in Dover, and they pulled them out of the high school and threw them into the war in Korea. I remember a kid up on Washington Street and he came back, shot up real bad.

When I was 11 or 12 years old I had a birthday. My father gave me a rifle for a birthday present—a brand new Winchester rifle. And we started a rifle club. And the whole idea was to teach all us kids how to fire a gun and how to be good shots with a rifle, because my father figured there was one war after another, we'd have to be prepared. When I was going to high school my father used to hunt a lot, so the house was always full of guns. We had to take gun training then to get a hunting permit. We'd go down and take a gun safety course.

In those days I can remember we were still riding bicycles. I wasn't driving in my early teens. I wanted to do some target shooting. So we'd get on the phone and call Chief of Police McCoy. We'd ask him if we could use the police range and he'd say, "Yes, sure, but you make sure you unload your guns before you go up Main Street." So we'd strap the rifles over our shoulder, get up on our bicycle, and ride up to the police range.

Right now, however, with people who haven't any association with guns, they're really scared to death of them. Nowadays if you have guns in the house you'll find your name on the front page of the newspaper as a terrorist. In those days everybody had guns. It was a matter of survival.

There'd probably be less trouble if there were more guns. Of course, we didn't have handguns. That causes most of the trouble.

I don't think it's a good thing to have to live under the stress of knowing you're going to be drafted and have to do your military service. I didn't go to college. I went to work, but I couldn't get a job and advance very far because everybody knew you were going to be drafted. You couldn't go anyplace. You couldn't plan anything. With all these things, as a kid you were living under tremendous tension.

What's not good is what you see today, these very unhealthy attitudes towards guns now. It probably wouldn't be a bad thing to give all kids gun training so they know how to stay out of trouble because all boys are interested in guns.

—Richard Boyd

We were in the union, and I paid my dues and all that stuff, and then the first week of July, [19]51, they came to us on a Saturday and they said, "As of today when you quit work at 11 o'clock," the foreman said, "Take all your belongings that you own"—the oil can, screw driver, pliers, the special shoes we wore that you got oil on. "On your way out, leave your address and telephone number and we'll call you when we start up again," he said.

They never called us. I was there for about 30 years. The next day it was Sunday and we couldn't get anyone from the union on the phone to ask them what the heck was going on. And our union leader said, "I don't know. You know as much as I do." And he went up to the bank to find out about our pension. Paul Fogel was the president of our union, the American Federation of Hosiery Workers, and he went up to the bank Monday morning to ask about the money for our pension. The bank said, "We're sorry. Your Pennsylvania office came in here with their lawyers and drew out all the money." Took every dime out. We lost everything that we put in there. Who are you gonna sue? Where are you gonna go? They moved south to Athens, Georgia, and Blue Ridge, Tennessee. I worked at Van Raalte for 32 years and I lost everything.

—Bill Mitchko

My mother was working doing slip covers for someone, a teacher, and she was renting space in this woman's house. The woman said, "You can go inside and cut the slip covers." Mom went in and on the bookshelves were nothing but Marx books, Communist catalogues, magazines, newspapers. She thought it was very peculiar. So she took some of the names down. When she went home she called the FBI. It was 1952, after the war. An FBI officer said, "I think you may have found something. Can you go back?" She said, "Yes, I have to deliver the slip covers." And he said, "Fine."

So she went back and a whole new set of books were there. She took down the names

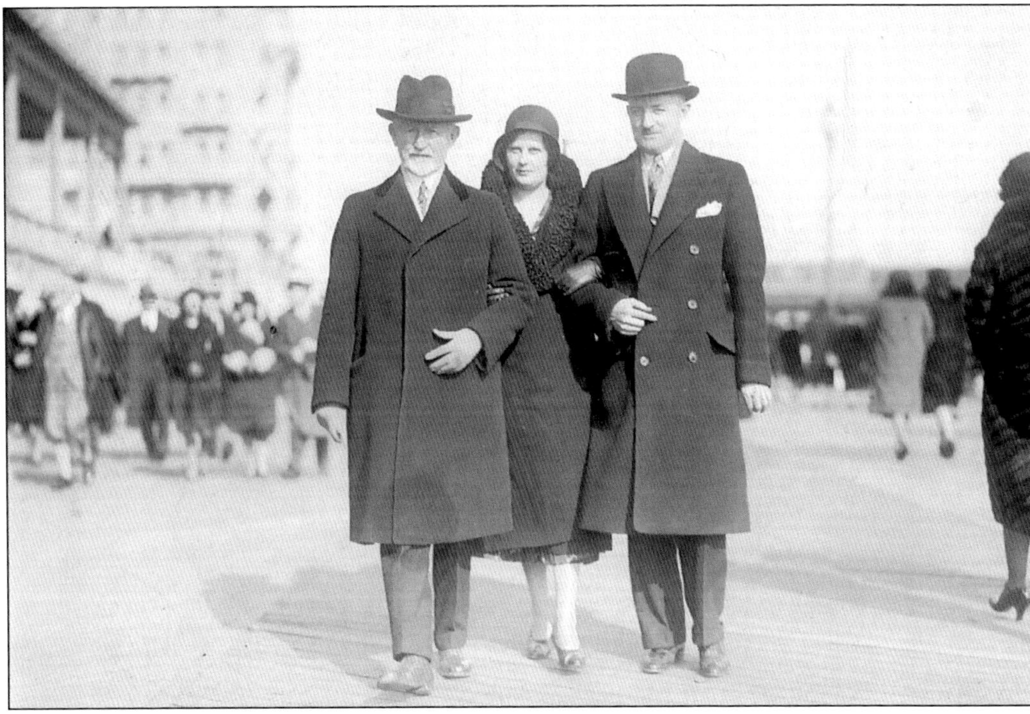

From left to right are Corita Forrest's great uncle Barney Burke; her mother, Marie Burke; and her father, Jack Burke. This picture was taken in Atlantic City c. *1932.*

of those and she called the FBI man and he said, "Thank you very much. You'll never hear from us again." And it was what they called a floating library, a Communist floating library that came to this woman's home, the woman who owned the house. And shortly after the woman was gone. And the poor woman who rented the apartment to her knew nothing about it. And the people in the neighborhood thought that she had rented it to a Communist.

I don't think she knew because she told my mother years later that she had no idea of this woman's background, or the books in her room.

People years ago were very narrow-minded. They're not as narrow-minded now as they used to be.

—Corita Forrest

The Janet Club started as a kind of joke. I was doing the newsletter "Nosy PARKer," and I got more and more involved in town projects. For some stupid reason I decided I would put musicians on Main Street for Christmas in the different stores. So I did.

One of the groups I was working with was the Boonton High School Alumni Chorus and Friends. And the girl who was the contact for that was Janet Middleton, and in the course of the arrangements, she said, "You know, you're the only other Janet I've met in my life." Then a few nights later, I began thinking there are so many Janets I know. There's Janet Marhefka, the police secretary and Janet Hess, who is the town's public health nurse. So in the next issue of our newsletter I listed all the Janets I knew in town and I said, "We ought to have a secret handshake and a magic decoder ring, and go out to lunch." So I contacted all the Janets I had listed.

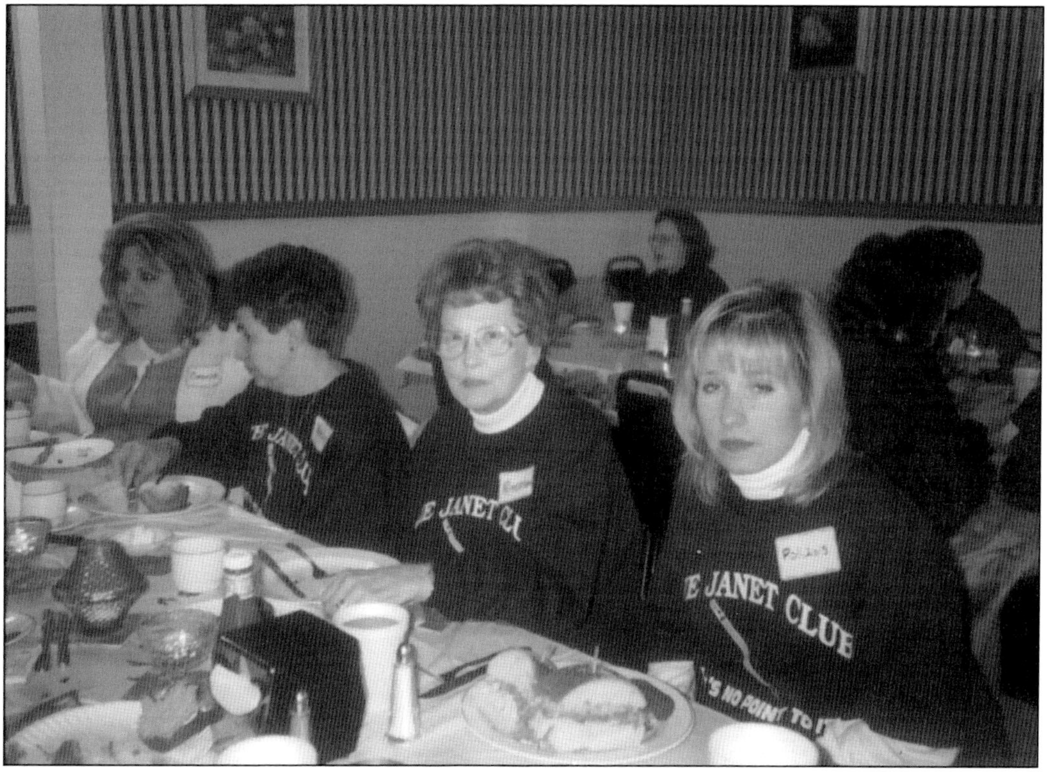

Monthly luncheon of the Janet Club at the Rivertop Deli. From left to right are Janet Toscano, Janet Bentley, Janet Peterson, and Janet Polizois.

We arranged to meet at the Rivertop Deli and there were seven or eight of us. I put out some publicity—silly publicity. The *Star-Ledger* picked it up; one of their reporters is Janet Proveromo.

I sent out letters and questionnaires to Janet celebrities—Janet Jackson, Janet Reno, Janet Leigh, Janet Guthrie, the racecar driver. Janet Reno sent her own questionnaire back immediately, handwritten. One question was "What kind of work do you do?" Her reply was "I do government work." Regardless of what anyone says about her politically, I give her a lot of points for that, because none of the others replied.

I designed a T-shirt and a sweatshirt with a "Janet Club" insignia. It has a yellow lead pencil on the front. And there's no point on it. And on the back of the T-shirt it says, "No agendas, no meetings, no committees." So there's no point to it. [Laughs.] It's still a lot of work. And all the members say, "Oh, this is so wonderful, to join a group in which I don't have to do anything."

We have Janets in about 26 states, several in England, two in Hong Kong. In the beginning people used to call and whisper, "Hellooo." I knew what was coming as soon as I heard that. "Hi, I'm Janet." And then some giggling.

At our last meeting, it was our third anniversary, I said "I think at the fifth anniversary, 2002, we should have an international gathering. We're making plans for that. Many of our Janets have music or performing backgrounds. So as part of this convention we'll do a show of our own with only Janet performers. I think that will be a kick in the head.

—Janet Bennett

EPILOGUE

The class of [19]48 had a 50th reunion recently, and quite a few of the people had stayed in town and a lot of them came from all over the country. They took photographs and put out a book of them, and items of those attending. When I looked at it I noticed that of all of those people, those that had moved away had aged the most. The ones that had stayed around town didn't seem to have aged; they looked much younger than they were. I mentioned that to somebody and she said, "What do you think it was, the air or the water?" And I said that if you hang around town people don't expect that much of you. When you move around there's more pressure and stress, and you have to bust your hump for it. But if you hang around town, you're just part of the scenery, you're part of the wallpaper, and one person looks like another. In the big cities you develop that anxious look about you, and everybody scurries.

—Jim Monaghan

Boonton was a blue-collar town because you had during the years the E.F. Drew Company [and] Boonton Molding, a major employer in the town. That's where a lot of the Pakistanian people came to [in] Boonton because the [onetime] president of Boonton Molding was . . . a Pakistanian and he brought his people over in the late [19]60s and early [19]70s, and that's when a lot of them started to come. They had a job and an ethnic group they could relate to. And you had the Carbone Company, which is still in Boonton.

Then you saw the closing of PBO, they went out of business. And the Boonton Molding and the pocketbook factory, and where my mother worked, Boonton Handbag, they did a lot for the war effort. They used to make the canteen pouches and [other] products.

So Boonton has changed over the years. It's not the industrial blue-collar town it was years ago. It's becoming more a commuting-type bedroom community. Years ago you walked to work. My grandfather worked at the Dawson Lumber Yard and walked to work, to put in his 8 or 10 hours. People today are living in Boonton and working in New York. Still, I think that hometown atmosphere is still here.

Years ago everybody did know everybody, whether you were up on the hill or living in the flats. One thing I found very interesting when I was the mayor and on the council is that Boonton had the largest senior citizen population of any town in Morris County. Something like 23 percent of the population in Boonton were senior citizens.

And I attribute that to people who had lived in Boonton, had lived there for generations. In the same house. And they remain in Boonton. I've always said that there must be a big magnet that lives on Main Street that keep us all here.

—Anthony Bucco

The old-fashioned way was that mothers and fathers would stay home. The trouble today is, in most cases, there's no parental supervision of the kids. The father works here and the mother works there. We had parental supervision all along, to tell us what was right and wrong. We were brought up right. And, of course, when I went to school, we had Bible reading and prayer every day in school.

Oh, that's prohibited now. So there was no source for the beginning of believing. If parents are not believers, the kids won't get a bit of it.

—Charles Bates

There's quite a King of the Hill going on with immigration. There is some feeling here about the Indian and Pakistani population because they bring their family in and then they bring in another family, and they all live in the same house. Well I've done my own family research. And the Irish coming in from Newfoundland did precisely the same thing, and I'm sure the Italians did the same thing.

What else can you do? You are not going to come here and buy a house. You may buy a gas station, which seems to be happening. I think what we're hearing is that "I got mine, now I'm going to make it hard for the new guys." I don't approve of that at all. People will say, "Why do they have to wear those outfits?" Well, if you went to India, would you immediately sell your jeans and buy Indian clothes? They buy them for the kids, because the kids are growing. They have to do it for the kids.

One of the things that intrigued me about Joe Marcello's book was that when the Italians first came here the merchants wouldn't deliver coal to them. In Boston, there were signs just like in the south, "No Irish need apply." It's always been like that. "I don't like you. You're different. I made it. Now get out of my way."

One side of my family is Irish. My mother denied it. Didn't want to know about it. And the other side is English. When somebody does a family history, you discover that nobody has bums in their family. Nobody. According to the author, their ancestors were all landowners. I always heard that my mother's grandfather was an English sea captain. Well he was a merchant seaman. When I researched it, you might be a mate on one trip and captain on another. It was rare that you were the top man all the time. And my great-great-grandfather was from Waterford, Ireland.

Well, my mother must have known that. But nope. According to my mother, they weren't Irish, they were English, because the Irish were not well thought of in Boston. It's fear.

—Janet Bennett

Years ago Boonton was a mom-and-pop-type organization. Everybody knew everybody. Everybody was kind to each other. It was mostly all Irish and Italian. There weren't many wealthy people and the wealthy people helped the poor. The Dunn girls were there, [and] their father Jack. In those days, long before me, they had big, horse-drawn carriages, and when people died they were put on a casket and carried up to the cemetery, Protestant and Catholic. . . . And if Jack Dunn wasn't there, he walked right behind. He believed that you should bury the dead. It's a proper work of mercy. He visited the sick, but he buried the dead.

The town of Boonton was really very nice. [The residents] looked out for each other. But now, progress, move on, and we find that we have a lot of empty stores. We don't have any delis, we don't have any shoemaker.

Janet Bennett's mother, Nina, and father, Leo, c. *1944.*

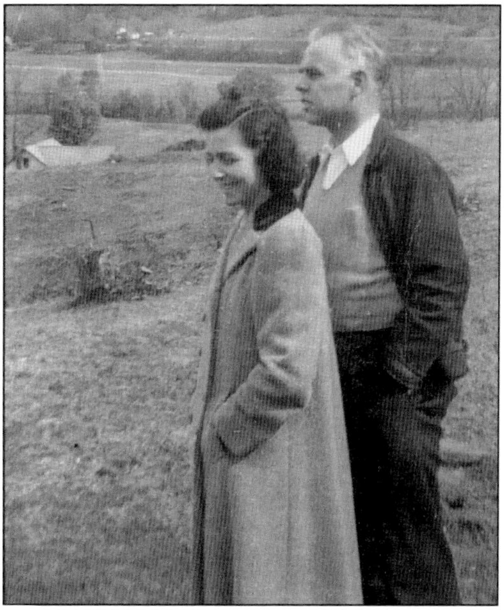

There were no problems with race relations years ago. There were no drugs. Oh, you had a couple of guys who went to the bars, barflies, alcoholics, but they were harmless characters. Today, my God! A lot has to do with TV. Part of it has to do with drugs. And the drugs are in the school system, and there's nothing much you can do about it. And our society has really deteriorated.

I mean the government is getting too much into things. I think we should be allowed to manage our own lives. Everything is being taken away gradually. If you had a job in Boonton, you had it for life. You were never competitive. Anybody who is under stress gets old much faster. It [was] not a dog-eat-dog situation in Boonton. But today it's a different situation. You walk on Main Street, you don't have the warm feeling you had years ago. Years ago, people would look out for you. In today's society with all the other elements on the outside, I don't think Boonton could survive. It's a way of life that's gone.

—Corita Forrest

Boonton was the trading center for this area. In the 1940s and early 1950s, there was nothing in Parsippany.

Parsippany was farmland. Montville was farmland. Morris County, Boonton, Butler, Morristown, and Dover [were] the four trading centers. You had to go to town to buy something. There were no stores on the highway. Boonton had a number of grocery stores. It had an A & P. It had an Acme.

On Main Street, Boonton always had problems with parking, but parking is not the problem today because there's always parking. All the storefronts are empty for economic reasons. First of all, taxes are too high. It's partially the town's problems. The taxes are too high for the rents they can get. The people who own those buildings must really be hurting because the storefronts are empty, and they've got to pay taxes to the town of Boonton.

Some of those storefronts are only 15 feet wide. But what you can't overcome is that you can't compete with the malls today. You can't do anything in retailing here. The places that survive now are antique shops, where they have antique shows, a sort of warehouse and showroom. They're open only certain days of the week. Anybody who has a mail-order business, they do all right.

Main Street today has to be recycled into other uses. But the town fathers seem incapable of doing that. They keep coming up with beautification programs. They want store owners to fix up their storefronts.

There was a big fight in town one time to get the town to put up decent lighting. The women used to be afraid of walking in the streets at night. So they spent a lot of money to put up this high-level mercury-vapor lighting up there. The poles were three stories high. They flooded the whole street with light. Just recently they went back and put back these old, 1890s [-style] Victorian lighting, and the streets suddenly got dark again. Beautification won't change economics, so they've got to do something. You've got to find other uses for those buildings.

—Richard Boyd

I don't like all the changes that are going on today. I'm in trouble with the police. They tell me I drive too much. And I say I do like hell. I don't live near a shopping mall. The closest place to shop is Boonton or Denville.

—Charles Bates

They're still children today just like they were 70 years ago. They have more opportunities now with the computers and all. But I really do think they're taking them out of early childhood too soon. They're growing up too fast.

In kindergarten we taught very little reading. I taught nature, music, art. I stressed etiquette. I was very close to the families and I still am. Today the teachers have to teach more reading and math, even in kindergarten. I think the little ones should grow up

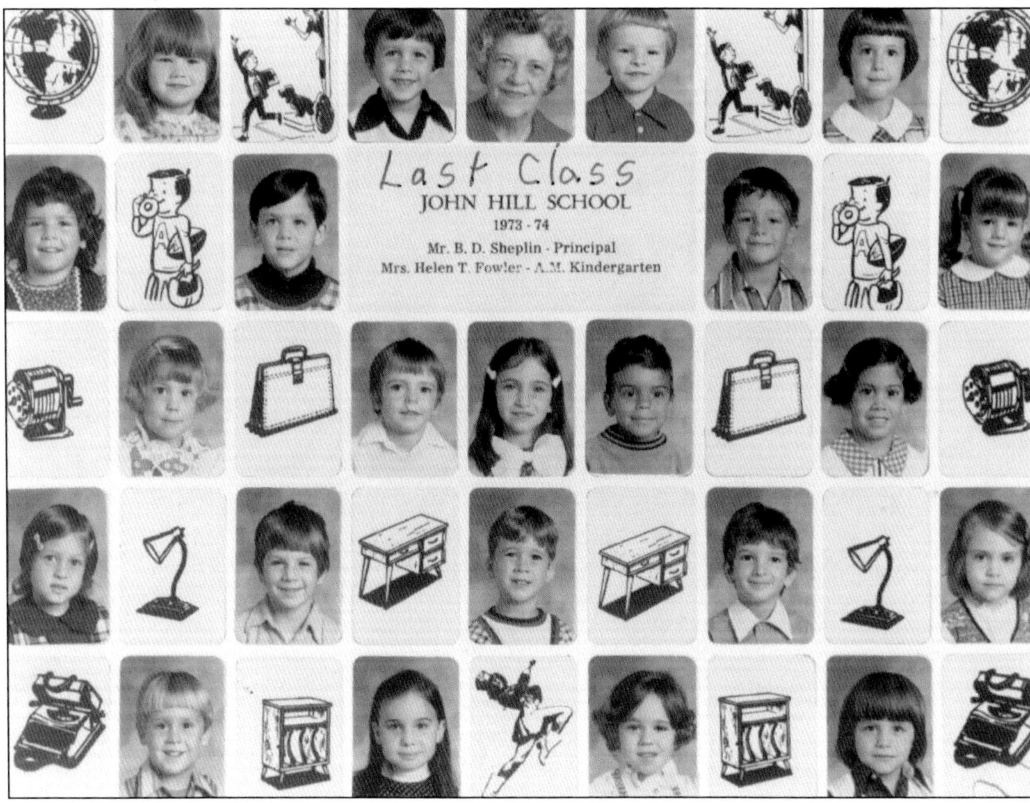

Pat Fowler's last class at the John Hill School, 1973–1974.

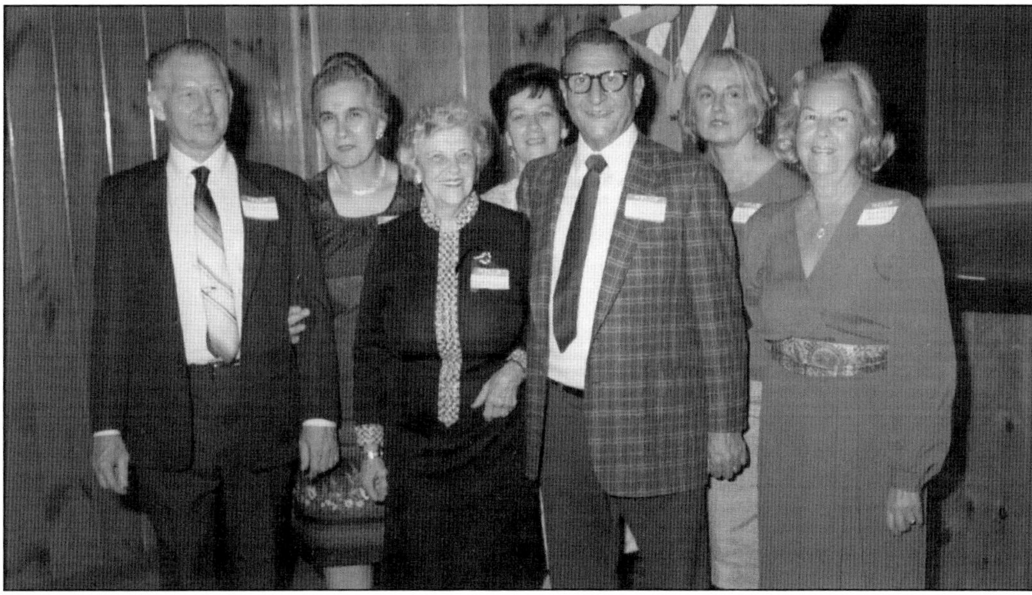

Reunion of Pat Fowler's kindergarten class of 1928.

more slowly. In fact I went to a luncheon where the state kindergarten director was speaking to us. She said, "Don't be pressured by your superintendent, your principals, and the children's family to teach reading. Those children may be mentally ready, but not emotionally." And she said, "They will find that those children who are being pushed so hard, when they get to high school and college, we're going to have more suicides. They'll be so emotionally upset." They've been pushed too fast. Today, mothers and fathers are demanding so much more of them, that the teachers have to do it.

I didn't do it. I'd take them on walks. We'd have the mothers with their children hiking out to the Rockaway Valley and Boonton Township to farms out there. They saw things in nature when they were little. Today, some of these children wouldn't even know what a cow looked like.

—Pat Fowler

I commuted from Rockaway to Boonton until I retired in [19]91 and that's when I moved back to Boonton. I work the polls. I belong to the Ecumenical Council. We have good rapport here. Mayor Edward Bolcar and I are good friends. I'm here where I'm doing things that I'm involved in. I'm vice-chair of the library board [and] chairperson with the housing authority. Right now I'm busy writing the history of the Bethel African-Methodist Episcopal Church on Plane Street.

We've made a lot of progress in the racial area. If there is discrimination now it's very subtle. All areas are very mixed. Before I came here Plane Street was where the blacks lived. Now it isn't true. They live all over Boonton, and they are part of everything that happens. The mayor recognized the black people who were influential in community affairs. He asked me to find these people and get them together.

When I retired, everyone wanted me to move either to Virginia or Ohio. But we were established here and we had friends, and we didn't want to leave. It's been very pleasant and one of things that has kept me young. [Laughs.]

—Louada Layton Ramsey

My entire philosophy is never to look back. You've got to make the best of whatever you have. You see, I've always been very realistic. I can fantasize as well as anyone else, but basically I'm very realistic. I think the army made me even more realistic, because things weren't going to happen the way you thought they were. It also taught me never to look back.

When I was 16 years old I wanted to be a missionary to China. By lots of people's standards I'm not very religious, but I have my own religious feelings. I've always believed in God, I've always thought He would take care of us. There was a plan here for you, and if you look for it, you can find it. And I have.

I am an enabler. People come to me with their problems and I try to find the place where they can get their problems solved. I won't tell you how to live your life, but I will try to tell them the place where they can go, or a person they can go to, who can help them solve their problems.

I've worked in human services in the county and I made myself knowledgeable about all the agencies in the county. And consequently I know people in every agency of the county to whom I can say, "Where can this person go?" And then I go back to see the people again. Lots of people tell you what to do, but I go back and see if they've done what they were supposed to do.

Greystone is so important to me because I think they've done such a poor job. There really is no reason why they should. Greystone is a mental hospital where people are committed by a judge because their cases are so severe. We have no idea how severe these cases are.

For two years they told me the swimming pool didn't work. Well, the swimming pool worked this year. I had to go to two or three of the top people, but the swimming pool is working. They got it fixed. I feel those people need help more than anyone else, and we do the least for them. The real problem is that nobody gives a hoot about them.

But whatever I do in the area of human relations, and much of it is tedious and sometimes hard work, it's, in many ways, my recreation. And it's been a godsend since my husband died.

—Jane Hopkins

You see it constantly in the papers. All of these towns wanting to protect and retain the atmosphere that was. And that, for the most part, [is what] the people who are moving there came for, and [they see] it evaporate in front of their eyes. When we moved here, we looked across that field. It had two enormous fir trees. We had grape vines and golden apples. We could look straight across to the Tourne. Kids played out in the field. This neighbor of ours extended his garden farther over and he grew vegetables every year. . . . And suddenly we have six houses.

It's still a nice town. It's up-scaling very rapidly and I don't think people are aware of that. It's a little scary for our age group. It's become a question of whether we will be able to live here anymore, because it will be too expensive.

People see some of the empty stores on Main Street filling up and they see progress. But what's filling up the stores bothers me. Not only the stores, but the buildings are being taken over by "tech" people. We have Web developers and service places. No new retail. And people are saying, "Isn't that wonderful? They're doing a good job, fixing up the buildings and the bank."

People who are coming to buy houses in Boonton are also buying the myth of the quaint town. And that's vanishing.

Another huge problem that nobody wants to put a name to is that there are too damn many of us. We do have to provide housing. There's too many people. We're reproducing like rabbits. And where are you going to put them? I don't know. On the other hand the people who are being the most destructive are the ones who are building these huge houses that they don't need. You don't need all that space. It's just ego. I don't know what the answer to any of . . . that is. I don't see that Boonton, internally, has changed a lot. There's an awful lot of new, younger people in town who are moving to Boonton because they like the old flavor, so they will perpetuate it. There's a couple down the street and they've got pictures of the house they just bought and what it used to be like, and in modernizing a long time ago the big front porch had been taken off. They're putting it back on. And that's happening a lot in Boonton, at the same time that some of this other stuff is going on. There's that tendency too. Granted, it's mythological. These Victorian houses were more like my house. It's a farmhouse, it's not "cutesy."

[In the past, there] was not the emphasis [on] pristine front yards. People who had a lot of money, with gardeners, had that stuff. A lot of the rest of us, we had grass. We didn't have lawns. You cut the grass. We didn't mow the lawn. And you used a scythe sometimes. The wonderful thing was "Music Man." That segment where he's trying to sell them the instruments, the clothes are hanging from the reel, hanging in her face, and she's sitting there. And every house had a galvanized tub leaning against the back door.

And bushel baskets. It was the way it was.

One thing that I think is happening is that Boonton is up-scaling very, very rapidly. And it's because of the location. The thing I complain about a lot is that there's some feeling in Boonton that we're not as good as Mountain Lakes, but we're defensive about it. And don't let anybody try to talk you out of it, because you'll get mad.

Someone in Boonton once said, and people used to get mad at it, "This is a blue-collar town and we like it that way." I think what he meant is "Don't tart us up." I think that's what a lot of people mean: "Look, we are who we are. Don't try to make us something else." That's why there was such an objection to putting the Victorian lights up, because this isn't a Victorian town at all. It was started in the 1830s and it was really like a frontier town. Victorian lights are a little too cute. They're very nice, but too affected.

—Janet Bennett

I think the young people of Boonton are very fine young boys and girls. They're not going to live the way we did. They're not going to have the same ideas, because they're in a different world altogether. But they're very good people. They grow up, have nice families, and work hard. We have many different nationalities now, more Spanish and Asian, but I think they contribute very well. Look at how these people graduate from school. Look at the list of graduates, and the colleges they've gone to. They're doing something right, because they're all getting into good colleges. And the ones that go to work, well that's not bad either. There are people who have to do that kind of work in the world. But judging from the ones I've met, they're very respectful. They don't have the same ideas we did, but we don't expect them to.

They've been exposed to a different world than the one we grew up in, and they're not going to react as we did. If we had lived at the time they're living in and we were watching some of these shows on television today we'd be different people too.

If you're sitting watching TV, and all that comes on isn't very nice or beneficial, you don't think it's bad, do you, if your parents are watching it. To us it's bad, and we're sorry it's being shown to young people, but how are you going to stop it? If you see it all the time, that becomes part of your life.

We watch the news every night. The Lehrer show, we always watch that one. I don't follow any sitcoms or anything like that. I'd much rather watch the ball games—baseball, golf—I like them all. I don't understand soccer. [Laughs.] There are so many good things on.

—Julia Dunn

ACKNOWLEDGMENTS

I want to thank Jean Merritt, Pam Geraldi Rabin, Allyn Meyers, Charles Geraldi, and the staff at the Boonton Historical Society and Boonton Holmes Public Library for their assistance on the book. A special thanks to Janet Bennett, who opened many doors to a Boonton I had not known. Her friendship and guidance gave me the opportunity to share the history of this unique town.

BIBLIOGRAPHY

"Artist-Life in the Highlands and Among the Nail-Makers." Reprinted from *Harper's New Monthly Magazine,* with an introduction by Robert R. Goller, Canal Society of New Jersey.

The Boonton Years, 1867 to 1967. Compiled for the Boonton Centennial Committee.

A History of Morris County, New Jersey.

Lee, James. *Tales the Boatmen Told.* Exton, Pennsylvania: Canal Press, 1977.

Lyon, Isaac S. *Lyon's Historical Discourse on Boonton,* Centennial Edition. Boonton Historical Society, 1967.

Macasek, Joseph J. *Guide to the Morris Canal.* The Morris County Heritage Commission, 1996.

Marcello, Joseph, Gary Marcello, and Ronald Marcello. *Life in Boonton, USA.* Dover, New Jersey: Direct Mail Services Inc., 1995.

Styple, William, and John J. Fitzpatrick, ed. *The Andersonville Diary and Memoirs of Charles Hopkins.* Kearny, New Jersey: Belle Grove Publishing Company, 1988.

Wendt, Peter C., Jr. *Boonton Was an Iron Town.* Boonton, New Jersey: Boonton Historical Society, 1976.

Willis, Charles E. *Scouts of '76.* Reprinted by Boonton Historical Society.

INDEX

Consistent with our mission to preserve history on a local level, this book was printed in South Carolina on American-made paper and manufactured entirely in the United States. Products carrying the accredited Forest Stewardship Council (FSC) label are printed on 100 percent FSC-certified paper.

MADE IN THE USA